Ninja Foodi Grill Cookbook for Beginners 2021-2022

1000 Days Quick & Delicious Indoor Grilling and Air Frying Recipes for Beginners and Advanced Users

Bridget Kieffer

Table of Contents

INTRODUCTION

The Ninja Foodi 5-in-1 Indoor Grill is an unbelievable and best multi-purpose cooking appliance. It can roast, air fry, bake, dry, and grill indoors. Poultry, Meat, vegetables, and fruit cookout very fine and complete juicy perfection. You can use the Ninja Foodi 5-in-1 Indoor Grill to make healthy food as well as snacks for your leisure time and parties. This unique appliance is a true gift for the BBQ lover as well as the foodie one.

Features of Ninja Foodi Grill

1. The unique Ninja Foodi Grill is Integrated Smart Probe. The grill sears, sizzles, and air fry crisps as well as mainly indoor grill and air fryer.

2. You can cook food with precision and quality and without generating smoke indoor.

3. The air circulates inside the Nin ja Foodi grill of about 500F on all sides of the grill.

4. The 500F air circulates all around the food for amazing crispiness and searing while the high-density grill creates amazing char-grilled marks and lovely flavors to food.

5. The Ninja Foodi Grill allows awesome control of setting: Low, Medium, High, and Max.

6. The wide temperature range of 105F500F and variable fan speed enable 5 fast, and versatile cooking functions: Grill, Air Crisp, Dehydrate, Roast, and Bake.

7. Air fry crisp with up to 75% less fat than deep-frying, using the included 4-qt crisper basket

8. No need to cut into foods or constantly probe them like when using an instant-read thermometer. Thus, you can eliminate guesswork and never worry about under or overcooking with the Integrated Smart Probe. Multi-task with peace of mind as food cooks to perfection

9. Instinctive digital display lets you easily choose a cooking function and see your food's internal temperature as the Integrated Smart Probe monitors it. The grill will conveniently help you when your food is perfectly cooked

10.   Virtually smoke-free with unique Smoke Control Technology. The combination of a temperature-controlled grill grate, splatter shield, and cool-air zone reduces smoke, keeping it out of the kitchen

Tips to Use Ninja Foodi Grill

When you are cooking for the first time with your Foodi grill, you must first wash the detachable cooking parts with warm soapy water to remove any oil and debris. Let air dry and place them back inside once you are ready to cook. An easy-to-follow instruction guide comes with each unit, so make sure to go over it before cooking.

Position your grill on a level and secure surface. Leaving at least 6 inches of space around it, especially at the back where the air intake vent and air socket are located. And you should ensure that the splatter guard is installed whenever the grill is in use. It is a wire mesh that covers the heating element on the inside of the lid.

1. Grilling. Plug your unit into an outlet and power on the grill. Use the grill grate over the cooking pot and choose the grill function. There are four default temperature settings of low at 400 degrees F, medium at 450 degrees F, high at 500 degrees F, and max at 510 degrees F. Set the time needed to cook. You may check the grilling cheat sheet that comes with your unit to guide you with the time and temperature settings. It is best to check the food regularly depending on the doneness you prefer and to avoid overcooking. Once the required settings are selected, press starts and waits for the digital display to show 'add food'. The unit will start to preheat similar to an oven and will show the progress through the display. This step takes about 8 minutes. If you need to check the food or flip it, the timer will pause and resume once the lid is closed. The screen will show 'Done' once the timer and cooking have been completed. Power off the unit and unplug the device. Leave the hood open to let the unit cool faster.

2. Bake. Remove the grates and use the cooking pot. Choose the bake setting and set your preferred temperature and time. Preheating will take about 3 minutes. Once done with preheating, you may put the ingredients: directly on the cooking pot, or you may use your regular baking tray. An 8-inch baking tray can fit inside as well as similar-sized oven-safe containers.

3. Roasting. Remove the grill grates and use the cooking pot that comes with the unit. You may also purchase their roasting rack for this purpose.

Press the roast option and set the timer between 1 to 4 hours according to the recipe requirements. The food will preheat for 3 minutes regardless of the time you have set.

Once ready, place the meat directly on the roasting pot or rack.

If you check the food occasionally for doneness. A meat thermometer is another useful tool to get your meats perfectly cooked.

4. Air crisping. Put the crisper basket in and close the lid. You should press the air crisp option and the start button. The default temperature is set at 390° F and will preheat at about 3 minutes. You can adjust the temperature and time by pressing the buttons beside these options.

If you do not need to preheat, just press the air crisp button a second time and the display will show you the 'add food' message. You should put the food inside and shake or turn it every 10 minutes. And you should use oven mitts or tongs with silicone when doing this.

5. Dehydrating. Place the first layer of food directly on the cooking pot. Add the crisper basket and add one more layer. Choose the dehydrate setting and set the timer between 7 to 10 hours. You can check the progress from time to time.

6.Cooking frozen foods. Choose the medium heat, which is 450° F using the grill option. You can also use the air crisp option if you are cooking fries, vegetables, and other frozen foods. Set the time needed for your recipe. Add a few minutes to compensate for the thawing.

Flip or shake after a few minutes to cook the food evenly.

Benefits of Ninja Foodi Grill on Health

1. Air fry crisp helps to maintain weight as it reduces 75% less fat than frying and has a 4 qt crisper basket.

2. There is no need to cut food as it cooks well and you will get healthy food all the time.

3. BBQ is always loved for ideal weight management and it allows you to manage a great diet and yummy food at the same time.

RECIPES WORTH TRYING

Peach BBQ Chicken Thighs

Prep Time: 15 minutes.
Cook Time: 15 minutes.
Serves: 6

Ingredients

- 4- 6 chicken thighs bone-in
- ¾ cup barbecue sauce
- 4 Tbsp peach preserve
- 1 ½ Tbsp Lemon Juice
- Salt and Pepper to taste

Preparation

1. Start by mixing peach preserves, barbecue sauce, lemon juice, and salt and pepper in a bowl. Whisk until well incorporated.
2. Place your chicken thighs in the marinade for 4 hours at a minimum.
3. Once chicken is done marinating, preheat your Ninja Foodi Grill. Toss chicken thighs on the grill, skin down.
4. Cook 4-5 minutes per side or until the chicken is nice and brown. Once get a nice grill mark on them, drop the heat down to medium.
5. Then finish cooking until the chicken reaches an internal temperature of 165 degrees F.
6. Remove chicken and place on a plate, and lightly cover with aluminum foil.
7. Let chicken rest 5 minutes before serving.

Serving Suggestion: Serve with salad on side.

Variation Tip: use vinegar instead of lemon.

Nutritional Information Per Serving:

Calories 342| Carbohydrates 15g | Protein 31g | Fat 18g | Sodium 639mg| Fiber 0g

Moroccan Roast Chicken

Prep Time: 5-10 minutes
Cook Time: 22 minutes
Servings: 4

Ingredients

- 3 tbsp plain yogurt
- 4 skinless, boneless chicken thighs
- 4 garlic cloves, chopped
- ½ tsp salt
- ⅓ cup olive oil
- ½ tsp fresh flat-leaf parsley, chopped

- 2 tsp ground cumin
- 2 tsp paprika
- ¼ tsp crushed red pepper flakes

Preparation

1. Take your food processor and add garlic, yogurt, salt, oil and blend as well.

2. Take a mixing bowl and add chicken, red pepper flakes, paprika, cumin, parsley, garlic, and mix well.

3. Let it marinate for 2-4 hours.

4. Pre-heat Ninja Foodi by pressing the "ROAST" option and setting it to "400 degrees F" and timer to 23 minutes.

5. Let it pre-heat until you hear a beep.

6. Arrange chicken directly inside your cooking pot and lock lid, cook for 15 minutes, flip and cook for the remaining time.

Serving Suggestion: Serve and enjoy with yogurt dip.

Variation Tip: use ranch sauce for extra flavor.

Nutritional Information per Serving:

Calories: 321| Carbohydrates: 6 g | Protein: 21 g | Fat: 24 g | Sodium: 602 mg |Fiber: 2 g

Greek Chicken with Tzatziki Sauce

Prep Time: 10 minutes.
Cook Time: 15 minutes.
Serves: 4

Ingredients

For the grilled chicken breasts:

- 4 chicken breasts
- ¼ cup extra-virgin olive oil
- 2 tsp dried oregano
- 1 tsp garlic powder
- Juice of one medium lemon
- Sea salt and freshly cracked pepper to taste

For the tzatziki sauce:

- ½ cup finely grated cucumber
- 1 cup of Greek yogurt
- 2 tsp of apple cider vinegar
- Juice of one medium lemon
- 1 tbsp of garlic powder

Preparation

1. For the chicken marinade, whisk together the lemon juice, olive oil, oregano, salt, pepper, and garlic powder in a medium bowl.

2. Pour into a Ziploc bag or container with the chicken to marinate in the refrigerator for at least 2 hours.

3. Meanwhile, make the tzatziki sauce by first grating the cucumbers.

4. Add in the Greek yogurt, vinegar, garlic, lemon juice, and sea salt to taste in a bowl. Chill in the refrigerator until ready to serve.

5. Heat up your Ninja Foodi Grill to 400 degrees.

6. Add the marinated chicken.

7. Cook the chicken breasts for about 5-7 minutes per side, depending on thickness. Remove from grill and allow the cooked chicken to rest.

Serving Suggestion: To serve, plate sliced chicken over a bed of rice top with the creamy tzatziki sauce and a lemon wedge. Enjoy!

Variation Tip: serve along with pita bread also.

Nutritional Information Per Serving:

Calories 521 | Carbohydrates 26g | Protein 59g | Fat 20g | Sodium 448mg| Fiber 2g

Juicy Stuffed Bell Peppers

Prep Time: 10 minutes

Cook Time: 15 minutes

Servings: 4

Ingredients

- 4 slices bacon, cooked and chopped
- 4 large eggs
- 1 cup cheddar cheese, shredded
- 4 bell peppers, seeded and tops removed
- Chopped parsley for garnish
- Salt and pepper to taste

Preparation

1. Divide cheese and bacon equally and stuff into your bell pepper.

2. Add eggs into each bell pepper. Season with salt and pepper.

3. Pre-heat your Ninja Foodi by pressing the "AIR CRISP" option and setting it to "390 Degrees F."

4. Set the timer to 15 minutes.

5. Let it pre-heat until you hear a beep.

6. Transfer bell pepper to your cooking basket and transfer to Ninja Foodi Grill.

7. Lock lid and cook for 10-15 minutes.

8. Cook until egg whites are cooked well until the yolks are slightly runny.

9. Remove peppers from the basket and garnish with parsley.

10. Serve and enjoy!

Serving Suggestion: Serve with parsley garnishing or enjoy as it is.

Variation Tip: use chopped dill for garnish.

Nutritional Information Per Serving:

Calories 326 | Carbohydrates 10g | Protein 22g | Fat 23g | Sodium 781mg| Fiber 2g

Steak Kabobs

Prep Time: 10 minutes.

Cook Time: 8 minutes.

Serves: 2

Ingredients

- 1-2 steaks
- 1 onion
- 1 bundle mushrooms
- 10-12 cherry tomatoes
- 1 bell pepper
- 2 - 2 ½ cup Italian Dressing
- Wooden or Metal Skewers

Preparation

- Cut steaks about 1-inch strips. Soak wooden skewers in water for at least 30 minutes. Or they will burn up.
- Pour Italian dressing over the steak and let it marinate while prep vegetables.
- Wash and prep vegetables.   The mushrooms whole and tomatoes whole and sliced the pepper and onions in around 1-inch pieces.
- Once skewers have been soaked in water, if using wood, start pushing steak and vegetables onto the skewers.
- Place in a dish and then pour the dressing over the top of the veggies and meat. Then cover and let marinate for 3-4 hours in the fridge.
- Preheat Ninja Foodi Grill. Select the grill setting and the highest heat. Let it preheat, it takes about 12 minutes.
- Once the grill is hot, carefully place your steak kabobs onto the grill. And you should cook 4-5 at a time.
- Close lid and select 8 minutes. Flip at the 4-minute mark.
- Cook steaks until it reaches your desired doneness. At 8 minutes our medium-well to well done. If you want rarer, cook for a bit less.
- Once your steak skewers are done, remove with tong, and then remove from skewers and serve.
- Enjoy these easy and delicious Ninja Foodi Grill steak kabobs any day of the week, and rain or shine.

Serving Suggestion: Serve delicious ranch sauce.

Variation Tip: use chicken and taste will be the same.

Nutritional Information Per Serving:

Calories 416 | Carbohydrates 17g | Protein 12g | Fat 33g | Sodium 1191mg| Fiber 1g

Minted Tomato, Onion & Glazed Tofu Kebabs

Prep Time: 15 minutes

Cook Time: 40 minutes

Servings: 4

Ingredients

- 1 14-ounce package extra-firm water-packed tofu, drained
- 1 tablespoon lime juice
- 16 fresh mint leaves
- 4 plum tomatoes, quartered and seeded
- 1 tablespoon reduced-sodium soy sauce
- 1 tsp minced fresh ginger
- 1 onion, peeled, quartered and separated into layers
- 2 jalapeño peppers, seeded and cut into ½-inch pieces
- ¼ cup Kecap manis

Preparation

1. Preheat the grill for eight minutes.

2. Cut the tofu in half horizontally, cutting two large slices about one inch thick. Take a kitchen towel and put it on the cutting board. Set the tofu on the towel. Put another clean folded towel over the tofu.

3. Put a flat and heavyweight thing like a skillet on top; Drain it for fifteen minutes; then remove the weight and cut the tofu into 1½-inch pieces.

4. Combine the lime juice, soy sauce, and ginger in a bowl. Add the tofu and toss it to coat. Cover it and marinate in the refrigerator for fifteen minutes.

5. Tuck in a mint leaf into every tomato quarter and thread them onto four or eight skewers alternatively with onion, tofu, and jalapenos.

6. Insert grill grate in the unit and close the hood. Select the option GRILL, set the temperature to LOW, and set time to ten minutes. Select the option START to begin preheating. .

Serving Suggestion: Serve with mint sauce.

Variation Tip: use lemon for tanginess.

Nutritional Information Per Serving:

Calories 412 | Carbohydrates 64.3g | Protein 16.1g | Fat 10.1g | Sodium 895mg| Fiber 2g

Chicken Satay

Prep Time: 40 minutes.

Cook Time: 6 minutes.

Serves: 3

Ingredients

- 1½ lbs chicken breast boneless, skinless

Marinade

- ½ cup coconut milk
- 2 cloves garlic minced
- 2" piece ginger grated
- 2 tsp turmeric
- 1 tsp sea salt
- 1 Tbsp Lemongrass Paste
- 1 Tbsp Chili Garlic Sauce
- 2 tsp Lemon Juice

Optional Garnishes

- chopped cilantro
- chopped peanuts
- peanut sauce

Preparation

1. If using bamboo skewers, soak them in water for at least 30 minutes before using.
2. Mix all the ingredients in the marinade in a medium size bowl.
3. Slice chicken breast into ½" strips and place into the marinade. Allow to marinate at room temp for 30 minutes.
4. Turn the Ninja Foodi Grill on and select the Grill function and MAX temp. Make sure the grilling grate that came with the grill is inside during the preheat. While the NF preheats, assemble your chicken skewers.
5. Take a strip and weave it onto a skewer.
6. When the Ninja Foodi Grill has preheated it will tell you to "add food." Add about 6 skewers to the grilling surface. Add more if they will fit, but don't overlap them or they won't cook evenly.
7. Close the lid and set the time for 6 minutes. Grill for 3 minutes and flip the skewers. Grill an additional 2-3 minutes
8. Garnish with fresh cilantro and chopped peanuts.

Serving Suggestion: serve with peanut sauce. Enjoy

Variation Tip: Add your favorite seasoning for taste.

Nutritional Information Per Serving:

Calories 177 | Carbohydrates 3g | Protein 25g | Fat 75g | Sodium 622mg| Fiber 1g

Steak and Potatoes

Prep Time: 15 minutes.
Cook Time: 45 minutes.
Serves: 4

Ingredients

- 3-4 potatoes russet
- 3 steak
- ¼ cup avocado oil
- 2 tbsp steak seasoning
- 1 tbsp sea salt

Preparation

1. Wash potatoes, dry, and poke with a fork all over them.
2. Rub avocado oil all over each one so they are well saturated. Sprinkle salt on outsides and put into air fryer basket.
3. Close lid and set to 400 degrees, air fryer function, for 35 minutes. Flip, then cook for an additional 10 minutes or until middle is fork tender when poked.
4. Remove potatoes and cover with foil to keep them warm. Remove air fryer basket and replace with grill piece inside machine. Close lid and set to grill, 500 degrees for 10 minutes. Allow to preheat.
5. Sprinkle both sides of steak with seasoning and press down so it sticks well.
6. When Ninja Foodi Grill is done preheating it will say lift adds food. Add steaks now.
7. Sirloins cooked 8 minutes flipping halfway through, filet cooked for 6 minutes flipping after 4 minutes.
8. Remove once you feel it is done to your liking. Allow to rest for at least 5 minutes to maintain juiciness before cutting.

Serving Suggestion: Serve with potatoes as side.

Variation Tip: use chopped dill for garnish.

Nutritional Information Per Serving:

Calories 572 | Carbohydrates 21g | Protein 38g | Fat 38g | Sodium 1849mg| Fiber 4g

BBQ Beef Short Ribs

Prep Time: 5 minutes.
Cook Time: 50 minutes.
Serves: 2

Ingredients

- 2 Beef Short Ribs
- ¼ c Red Wine
- ¾ c Beef Stock
- ¼ c Diced Onion

- ½ c BBQ sauce

Seasoning
- Seasoning salt
- Garlic Powder
- Onion Powder
- 1 Tbsp Cornstarch

Preparation

1. Season the beef ribs with the seasonings.
2. Add the onion, wine, and broth to the bottom of the Foodi cooking bowl.
3. Close the toggle switch to sealing.
4. Pressure cook on manual, high, for 40 minutes.
5. Do a natural release for 10 minutes, and then carefully release any remaining pressure until the pin drops and its safe open the lid.
6. Remove the ribs to a plate.
7. Generously brush the BBQ sauce over the entire surface of the ribs. Place the ribs back into the pot, on the top rack of the air crisping rack.
8. Air crisps the ribs for 10 minutes. Feel free to flip them halfway through.
9. Remove the ribs to rest and take out the rack.
10. Mix up the slurry and pour into the pan juices in the pot to thicken.
11. Spoon over the ribs and enjoy!

Serving Suggestion: Serve warm with slurry.

Variation Tip: use chicken drumsticks as same but avoid pressure cook.

Nutritional Information Per Serving:
Calories 906 | Carbohydrates 78g | Protein 50g | Fat 22g | Sodium 2667mg| Fiber 3g

Chicken & Bacon Caesar Salad

Prep Time: 35 minutes.
Cook Time: 30 minutes.
Serves: 4

Ingredients

Marinated Chicken Breasts
- 1 lb chicken breasts
- ⅛ cup balsamic vinegar
- ⅛ cup olive oil
- ¼ tsp garlic powder
- ¼tsp black pepper
- ¼ tsp salt

Caesar Dressing
- ⅔ cup mayo
- 4 anchovies in oil

- 2 small cloves garlic
- 2.5 tbsp lemon juice
- 2 tbsp nutritional yeast
- ½ tsp dijon mustard
- ½ tsp coconut amino
- ¼ tsp apple cider vinegar
- ½ tsp salt
- ¼ tsp pepper

Salad & Toppings

- 8 cups romaine lettuce
- 4 eggs soft or hard boiled
- 8 oz. sugar free bacon cooked
- 1 tsp nutritional yeast

Preparation

1. Prepare the Chicken Breasts: Put one chicken breast inside a zip lock bag Gently pound the chicken using a meat tenderizer or heavy rolling pin until it's even in thickness. Repeat for the other chicken breasts.

2. Whisk together the marinade ingredients and pour it over the chicken, turning to coat. Marinate for 30-60 minutes.

3. Turn your grill to medium and allow preheating. Add the chicken breasts to the grill, cooking for about 12 minutes, turning once. Remove from the heat and let the chicken on the rest before slicing.

4. **Prepare the Salad Toppings**: Wash and chop the lettuce. Cook the bacon and allow it to cool, and then roughly chop it. Boil the eggs however you like them and slice them into halves or quarters.

5. **Make the Caesar Salad Dressing:** Using an immersion blender set to low, mix together all the ingredients, smash the garlic clove and finely chop the anchovies, then whisk all ingredients together in a bowl.

6. Season to taste with salt and pepper. Keep it covered in the refrigerator for up to 5 days.

7. **Assemble the Salad:** Divide the lettuce among four large bowls. Top each bowl with nutritional yeast, salad dressing, chicken, eggs, and bacon.

8. Sprinkle each salad with cracked black pepper and enjoy.

Serving Suggestion: Serve with dill garnishing or enjoy as it is.

Variation Tip: For a low carb / keto option, simply omit the tomatoes.

Nutritional Information Per Serving:

Calories 631 | Carbohydrates 12g | Protein 42g | Fat 46g | Sodium 1461mg| Fiber 3g

Ninja Foodi Grill Steak

Prep Time: 5 minutes.
Cook Time: 7 minutes.
Serves: 2

Ingredients

- 2 steaks
- 1 tbsp kosher salt
- ¼ tsp corn starch
- ½tsp chili powder
- 2 tsp brown sugar
- ¼tsp onion powder
- 1 tsp black pepper
- ¼ tsp Turmeric
- ½ tsp smoked paprika

Preparation

1. Mix up all steak seasonings in a bowl.
2. Once steaks are rubbed down with the spices on all sides, wrap or cover and store in the fridge. Store for 30 minutes to 2 hours.
3. Preheat your Ninja Foodi Grill to the highest grill setting and allow it to fully preheat. It takes about 8-12 minutes.
4. Once the preheat is done take your steaks and place them on the grill.
5. You will cook your steaks to the doneness you desire.
6. Once steaks are done, allow resting on a plate for 5 minutes that is tented in aluminum foil.

Serving Suggestion: Serve with grilled veggies as side.

Variation Tip: differ seasoning allows unique taste.

Nutritional Information Per Serving:

Calories 319 | Carbohydrates 3g | Protein 29g | Fat 21g | Sodium 1654mg| Fiber 0g

Carne Asada Street Tacos

Prep Time: 3 minutes.
Cook Time: 20 minutes.
Serves: 8

Ingredients

- 2 tsp sea salt
- 2 tsp cumin
- 2 tsp smoked paprika
- 1 tsp garlic powder
- 1 tsp onion powder
- ¼ tsp chipotle
- ½ cup orange juice fresh squeezed
- ¼ cup lime juice
- 4 garlic cloves about ½ Tbsp

- 1 Ancho chili pepper dry
- 1 cup cilantro I use the stems

Carne Asada

- 1 ½ pounds skirt steak
- 1 cup beef stock
- 16 corn tortillas
- 4 ounces cotija cheese
- Cilantro for garnish
- ½ cup radishes sliced.
- 1 cup onion diced

Preparation

1. Mix up the spices and add to a medium size sealable bag.
2. Slice the steak against the grain into thin strips and place into baggy with the dry spices. Shake to coat meat and then add the remaining marinade ingredients. Leave at room temp for 30 minutes or refrigerate for 4 hours or overnight.
3. Dump the steak and the marinade into the inner pot. Add 1 cup of beef stock. Set the pressure on high for 10 minutes. Allow the Ninja Foodi to release its pressure for 10 minutes then immediately release the remaining pressure.
4. Put the rack in the high position and lay the corn tortillas over 2 rungs in the rack. Spritzing with oil will help them be more pliable.
5. Turn the broil on for 3 minutes or until they become warm and slightly crispy.
6. Double the corn tortillas and stuff with carne a Sada meat and top with crumbled cheese, cilantro, onion, and sliced radishes. Serve & Enjoy!

Serving Suggestion: Serve with your favorite dipping sauce.

Variation Tip: use chopped dill for garnish.

Nutritional Information Per Serving:

Calories 308 | Carbohydrates 34g | Protein 24g | Fat 9g | Sodium 731mg| Fiber 5g

Grilled Huli Huli Chicken

Prep Time: 5 minutes.
Cook Time: 12 minutes.
Serves: 8

Ingredients

- 6-8 Chicken Legs
- ½ tsp fresh ginger, minced or crushed
- 1 tsp garlic, minced or crushed
- ¼ cup brown sugar
- 3 Tbsp ketchup
- 4 Tbsp soy sauce
- 2 Tbsp chicken stock, as needed

Preparation

1. In a bowl, add ketchup, soy sauce, garlic, ginger, and brown sugar. Mix well and slowly add in the chicken stock. thin up the marinade a bit to make it easier to cover the chicken.

2. In a container or bag add your chicken legs and pour ½ of the marinade sauce all over the chicken. Cover and let marinate at least 2 hours to overnight.

3. Once the chicken is marinated, preheat your Ninja Foodi Grill or another grill to high heat. When it hot toss your chicken legs on, leaving space between each.

4. Cook 4-6 minutes on each side, basting with the remaining marinade. Cook until the internal temperature reaches 165 degrees internal temperature.

5. Remove the Huli Huli chicken from the grill, let the rest 5 minutes then serve with your favorite sides.

Serving Suggestion: Serve with mashed potatoes or grilled veggies as side.

Variation Tip: use chopped cilantro for garnish.

Nutritional Information Per Serving:

Calories 509 | Carbohydrates 8g | Protein 63g | Fat 23g | Sodium 752mg| Fiber 0g

Grilled Chicken Bruschetta

Prep Time: 10 minutes.
Cook Time: 15 minutes.
Serves: 3

Ingredients

- 3 Chicken Breasts
- Roasted Garlic and Bell Pepper Seasoning
- Salt and Pepper, to taste
- Cooking Oil Spray for Grill
- 1 cup Basil Pesto
- Fresh Mozzarella Cheese, Sliced
- 2 Roma Tomatoes, diced

Preparation

1. Place the chicken in gallon size bag and then use a meat mallet to pound the chicken to around ¼" thick.

2. Remove from bag and place raw chicken on a platter and season with the Roasted Garlic and Bell Pepper Seasoning.

3. For the Ninja Foodi Grill select the air fryer setting and do 425 and cook to broil the cheese and brown it up. Otherwise toss it right in the oven on broil for 2-4 minutes or until the cheese is browned and melted.

4. Place some pesto on top of each chicken breast, then slice and lay out some fresh mozzarella on each slice of chicken.

5. Remove your grilled bruschetta chicken from the oven and top with diced roma tomatoes, add extra pesto, basil leaves and serve as desired.

Serving Suggestion: Serve with diced tomatoes.

Variation Tip: use salt and pepper for seasoning and it taste yummy.

Nutritional Information Per Serving:

Calories 359 | Carbohydrates 6g | Protein 25g | Fat 5g | Sodium 399mg| Fiber 1g

Marinated London Broil

Prep Time: 5 minutes.

Cook Time: 8 minutes.

Serves: 4

Ingredients

- 1 ½ lbs London Broil
- ¼ cup red wine vinegar
- 1 Tbsp olive oil
- 1½ Tbsp spicy mustard
- 2 cloves garlic minced
- 1 Tbsp Worcestershire sauce
- 1-2 tsp rosemary fresh
- 1 tsp sea salt
- 1 tsp onion powder
- 1 tsp dried thyme
- ½ tsp black pepper

Preparation

1. Tenderize each side with a meat tenderizer.
2. Mince the garlic cloves and finely chop the rosemary. Combine all the marinade ingredients into a large plastic, sealable bag. Add the steak and seal the bag. Mix the marinade all around so the ingredients combine with each other. Then squeeze the air out of the bag and refrigerate for 2-4 hours.
3. Remove the steak from the fridge, leave it in the bag and let it sit at room temp for 30 minutes.
4. Remove the steak from the bag and blot off the marinade.
5. Preheat the grill on max grill. When it says "ADD FOOD" lays the steak on the grill surface and presses the steak down onto the grill surface.
6. Grill on max grill for 4 minutes and then flip. Grill on max grill another 2-4 minutes for medium rare. Remove from grill and let the steak rest for 5-10 minutes.

Serving Suggestion: Slice thinly across the grain. Serve & Enjoy!

Variation Tip: use fresh herbs.

Nutritional Information Per Serving:

Calories 265 | Carbohydrates 2g | Protein 40g | Fat 9g | Sodium 798mg| Fiber 1g

Homely Zucchini Muffin

Prep Time: 5-10 minutes

Cook Time: 7 minutes

Servings: 4

Ingredients

- 4 whole eggs
- 1 zucchini, grated
- 2 tbsp almond flour
- ½ tsp salt
- 1 tsp butter

Preparation

1. Add zucchini, salt, and almond flour into a mixing bowl.

2. Mix them well.

3. Grease muffin molds with butter.

4. Add zucchini mixture to them.

5. Arrange muffin tins in your Ninja Foodi Grill.

6. Then close the lid and cook on "Air Crisp" mode for 7 minutes at 375 degrees F.

Serving Suggestion: Serve warm with tea.

Variation Tip: use cheese inside the muffin for fun.

Nutritional Information per Serving:

Calories: 94| Fat: 8 g| Carbohydrates: 2 g| Fiber: 0.5 g| Sodium: 209 mg| Protein: 7 g

Ninja Foodi Bean

Prep Time: 5 minutes

Cook Time: 10 minutes

Servings: 4

Ingredients

- Fresh ground black pepper
- Flaky sea salt
- Pinch of pepper
- 1 lemon, juiced
- 2 tablespoon oil
- 1-pound green bean, trimmed

Preparation

1. Take a medium bowl and add the green bean.

2. Mix and stir well.

3. Preheat your Ninja Foodi Grill to MAX and set the timer to 10 minutes.

4. Wait until you hear a beep. Transfer beans to the grill grate, cook for 8-10 minutes.

5. Toss well to ensure that all sides cooked evenly.

6. Squeeze a bit of lemon juice on the top.

7. Season with salt, pepper and pepper flakes according to your taste.

8. Enjoy!

Serving Suggestion: Serve with bread.

Variation Tip: use chopped dill for garnish.

Nutritional Information Per Serving:

Calories 100 | Carbohydrates 10g | Protein 2g | Fat 7g | Sodium 30mg| Fiber 4g

Kale and Sausage Delight

Prep Time: 10 minutes

Cook Time: 10 minutes

Servings: 4

Ingredients

- Olive oil as needed
- 1 cup mushrooms
- 2 cups kale, fine chopped
- 4 sausage links
- 4 medium eggs
- 1 medium yellow onion, sweet

Preparation

1. Open the lid of your Ninja Foodi Grill and arrange the Grill Grate.

2. Pre-heat your Ninja Foodi Grill to HIGH and set the timer to 5 minutes.

3. Once you hear the beeping sound, arrange sausages over the grill grate.

4. Cook for 2 minutes, flip and cook for 3 minutes more.

5. Take a baking pan and spread out the kale, onion, mushroom, sausage and crack an egg on top. Cook on BAKE mode on 350 degrees F for about 5 minutes more.

6. Serve and enjoy!

Serving Suggestion: Serve with bread.

Variation Tip: use fresh baked vegetables as side.

Nutritional Information Per Serving:

Calories 236 | Carbohydrates 17g | Protein 18g | Fat 12g | Sodium 369mg| Fiber 4g

Energetic Bagel Platter

Prep Time: 5-10 minutes

Cook Time: 8 minutes

Servings: 4

Ingredients

- 4 bagels, halved
- 2 tbsp coconut flakes
- 1 cup fine sugar
- 2 tbsp black coffee, prepared and cooled down
- ¼ cup of coconut milk

Preparation

1. Take your Ninja Foodi Grill and open the lid.

2. Arrange grill grate and close top.

3. Pre-heat Ninja Foodi by pressing the "GRILL" option and setting it to "MEDIUM.".

4. Set the timer to 8 minutes.

5. Let it pre-heat until you hear a beep.

6. Arrange bagels over grill grate and lock lid.

7. Cook for 2 minutes.

8. Flip sausages and cook for 2 minutes more.

9. Repeat the same procedure to grill remaining Bagels.

10. Take a mixing bowl and mix the remaining Ingredients Pour the sauce over grilled bagels

11. Serve and enjoy!

Serving Suggestion: Serve with sauce.

Variation Tip: add fried egg for taste.

Nutritional Information Per Serving:

Calories 300 | Carbohydrates 42g | Protein 18g | Fat 23g | Sodium 340mg| Fiber 4g

Butternut Squash with Italian Herbs

Prep Time: 5-10 minutes

Cook Time: 16 minutes

Servings: 4

Ingredients

- 1 medium butternut squash, peeled, seeded, and cut into ½ inch slices
- 1 tsp dried thyme
- 1 tablespoon olive oil
- 1 and ½ tsp oregano, dried
- ¼ tsp black pepper

- ½ tsp salt

Preparation

1. Add all the Ingredients into a mixing bowl and mix it.

2. Pre-heat your Ninja Foodi by pressing the "GRILL" option and setting it to "MED.".

3. Set the timer to 16 minutes.

4. Allow it to pre-heat until you hear a beep.

5. Arrange squash slices over the grill grate.

6. Cook for 8 minutes.

7. Flip them and cook for 8 minutes more.

8. Serve and enjoy!

Serving Suggestion: Serve with your favorite drink.

Variation Tip: use chopped dill for garnish.

Nutritional Information Per Serving:

Calories 238 | Carbohydrates 36g | Protein 158g | Fat 12g | Sodium 128mg| Fiber 3g

Mushroom Pepper

Prep Time: 10 minutes

Cook Time: 10 minutes

Servings: 4

Ingredients

- 4 cremini creminis mushrooms, sliced
- 4 large eggs
- ½ cup cheddar cheese, shredded
- ½ onion, chopped
- ¼ cup whole milk
- Sea salt
- ½ bell pepper, seeded and diced
- Black pepper

Preparation

1. Add eggs and milk into a medium bowl.

2. Whisk them together.

3. Add mushrooms, onion, bell pepper, and cheese.

4. Mix them well.

5. Preheat by selecting the "BAKE" option and setting it to 400 degrees F.

6. Set the timer for 10 minutes.

7. Pour the egg mixture into the baking pan and spread evenly.

8. Let it pre-heat until you hear a beep.

9. Then close the lid.

10. Cook for 10 minutes.

11. Serve and enjoy!

Serving Suggestion: Serve and enjoy.

Variation Tip: add melted cheese for extra flavor.

Nutritional Information Per Serving:

Calories 153 | Carbohydrates 5g | Protein 11g | Fat 10g | Sodium 494mg| Fiber 1g

Stuffed up Bacon and Pepper

Prep Time: 10 minutes

Cook Time: 15 minutes

Servings: 4

Ingredients

- Chopped parsley, for garnish
- Salt and pepper to taste
- 4 whole large eggs
- 4 bell pepper, seeded and tops removed
- 4 slices bacon, cooked and chopped
- 1 cup cheddar cheese, shredded

Preparation

1. Take the bell pepper and divide the cheese and bacon evenly between them.

2. Crack eggs into each of the bell pepper.

3. Season the bell pepper with salt and pepper.

4. Pre-heat your Ninja Food Grill in AIR CRISP mode with temperature to 390 degrees F.

5. Set timer to 15 minutes.

6. Once you hear the beep, transfer the bell pepper to cooking basket.

7. Transfer your prepared pepper to Ninja Foodi Grill and cook for 10-15 minutes until the eggs are cooked, and the yolks are just slightly runny.

Serving Suggestion: Serve, Garnish with a bit of parsley.

Variation Tip: use chopped dill for garnish.

Nutritional Information per Serving:

Calories: 326| Fat: 23 g| Carbohydrates: 10 g| Fiber: 2 g| Sodium: 781 mg| Protein: 22 g

Epic Breakfast Burrito

Prep Time: 5-10 minutes

Cook Time: 30 minutes

Servings: 4

Ingredients

- 12 tortillas
- Salt and pepper to taste

- 2 cups potatoes, diced
- 3 cups cheddar cheese, shredded
- 10 whole eggs, beaten
- 1 pound breakfast sausage
- 1 tsp olive oil

Preparation

1. Pour olive oil into a pan over medium heat.

2. Cook potatoes and sausage for 7 to 10 minutes, stirring frequently.

3. Spread this mixture on the bottom of the Ninja Foodi Grill pot.

4. Season with salt and pepper.

5. Pour the eggs and cheese on top.

6. Select bake setting. Cook at 325 degrees F for 20 minutes.

7. Top the tortilla with the cooked mixture and roll.

8. Sprinkle cheese on the top side. Add Crisper basket to Ninja Foodi Grill.

9. AIR CRISP the Burritos for 10 minutes at 375 degrees F.

10. Serve and enjoy!

Serving Suggestion: Serve with your favorite sauce.

Variation Tip: use variation with vegetables.

Nutritional Information Per Serving:

Calories: 400| Fat: 20 g| Carbohydrates: 36 g| Fiber: 5 g| Sodium: 675 mg| Protein: 22 g

Simple Zucchini Egg Muffins

Prep Time: 5-10 minutes

Cook Time: 7 minutes

Servings: 4

Ingredients

- 4 whole eggs
- 2 tbsp almond flour
- 1 zucchini, grated
- 1 tsp butter
- ½ tsp salt

Preparation

1. Take a small-sized bowl and add almond flour, salt, zucchini. Mix well.

2. Take muffin molds and grease them gently, add the zucchini mix.

3. Arrange your molds in Ninja Foodi Grill and cook on "AIR CRISP" mode for 7 minutes at a temperature of 375 degrees F.

4. Serve and enjoy the meal once complete!

Serving Suggestion: Serve in breakfast.

Variation Tip: Add mushroom for taste.

Nutritional Information per Serving:

Calories: 94|Fat: 8 g| Carbohydrates: 2 g| Fiber: 0.5 g| Sodium: 209 mg |Protein: 7 g

The Broccoli and Maple Mix

Prep Time: 5-10 minutes

Cook Time: 10 minutes

Servings: 4

Ingredients

- 2 heads broccoli, cut into florets
- 4 tbsp soy sauce
- 2 tsp maple syrup
- 4 tablespoons balsamic vinegar
- 2 tsp canola oil
- Red pepper flakes and sesame seeds for garnish

Preparation

1. Take a shallow mixing bowl and add vinegar, soy sauce, oil, maple syrup.

2. Whisk the whole mixture thoroughly.

3. Add broccoli to the mix.

4. Keep it aside. Set your Ninja Foodi Grill to "MAX" mode.

5. Set the timer to 10 minutes.

6. Once you hear the beep, add prepared broccoli over Grill Grate.

7. Cook for 10 minutes.

8. Serve and enjoy!

Serving Suggestion: Serve topped with sesame seeds, pepper flakes.

Variation Tip: use your favorite vegetables.

Nutritional Information per Serving:

Calories: 141| Fat: 7 g, Fat: 1 g, Carbohydrates: 14 g, Fiber: 4 g, Sodium: 853 mg, Protein: 4 g

Veggie Packed Egg Muffin

Prep Time: 5-10 minutes

Cook Time: 7 minutes

Servings: 4

Ingredients

- 4 whole eggs
- 2 tbsp almond flour
- 1 tsp butter
- 1 zucchini, grated
- ½ tsp salt

Preparation

1. Add almond flour, zucchini, and salt into a mixing bowl.

2. Mix them well.

3. Grease muffin molds with butter.

4. Adds zucchini mixture to them.

5. Arrange muffin tins in your Ninja Foodi Grill and lock the lid.

6. Cook on "Air Crisp" mode for 7 minutes at 375 degrees F.

Serving Suggestion: Serve warm.

Variation Tip: use chopped dill for taste.

Nutritional Information per Serving:

Calories: 94| Fat: 8 g| Carbohydrates: 2 g| Fiber: 0.5 g| Sodium: 209 mg| Protein: 7 g

Morning Frittata

Prep Time: 10 minutes

Cook Time: 10 minutes

Servings: 4

Ingredients

- 4 large eggs
- 4 c cremini mushrooms, sliced
- ½ bell pepper, seeded and diced
- ½ cup shredded cheddar cheese
- ½ onion, chopped
- ¼ cup whole milk
- Salt and pepper to taste

Preparation

1. Add eggs and milk into a medium-sized bowl.
2. Whisk it and then season with salt and pepper.
3. Then add bell pepper, onion, mushroom, cheese. Mix them well.
4. Pre-heat Ninja Foodi by pressing the "BAKE" option and setting it to "400 Degrees F."
5. Set the timer to 10 minutes.
6. Let it pre-heat until you hear a beep.
7. Pour Egg Mixture in your Ninja Foodi Bake Pan, spread well.
8. Transfer to Grill and lock lid.
9. Bake for 10 minutes until lightly golden.
10. Serve and enjoy!

Serving Suggestion: Serve warm with tea.

Variation Tip: use your favorite vegetables for taste.

Nutritional Information per Serving:

Calories: 153| Fat: 10 g| Carbohydrates: 5 g| Fiber: 1 g| Sodium: 177 mg| Protein: 11 g

DELICIOUS CHICKEN AND POULTRY

Grilled BBQ Turkey

Prep Time: 5-10 min.

Cook Time: 30 min.

Servings: 5-6

Ingredients

- ½ cup minced parsley
- ½ cup chopped green onions
- 4 garlic cloves, minced
- 1 cup Greek yogurt
- ½ cup lemon juice
- 1 tsp dried rosemary, crushed
- ⅓ cup canola oil
- 4 tbsp minced dill
- 1 tsp salt
- ½ tsp pepper
- 1-3 pounds turkey breast half, bone in

Preparation

1. In a mixing bowl, combine all the Ingredients except the turkey. Add and coat the turkey evenly. Refrigerate for 8 hours to marinate.

2. Take Ninja Foodi Grill, arrange it over your kitchen platform, and open the top lid.

3. Arrange the grill grate and close the top lid.

4. Press "GRILL" and select the "HIGH" grill function. Adjust the timer to 30 minutes and then press "START/STOP." Ninja Foodi will start pre-heating.

5. Ninja Foodi is preheated and ready to cook when it starts to beep. After you hear a beep, open the top lid.

6. Arrange the turkey over the grill grate.

7. Close the top lid and cook for 15 minutes. Now open the top lid, flip the turkey.

8. Close the top lid and cook for 15 more minutes. Cook until the food thermometer reaches 350°F.

9. Slice and serve.

Serving Suggestion: Serve with grill veggies.

Variation Tip: add red pepper flakes for spiciness.

Nutritional Information per Serving:

Calories: 426|Fat: 8.5g| Carbohydrates: 22g| Fiber: 3g| Sodium: 594mg| Protein: 38g

Sweet and Sour Chicken BBQ

Prep Time: 10 minutes

Cook Time: 40 minutes

Servings: 4

Ingredients

- 6 chicken drumsticks
- ¾ cup of sugar
- 1 cup of soy sauce
- 1 cup of water
- ¼ cup garlic, minced
- ¼ cup tomato paste
- ¾ cup onion, minced
- 1 cup white vinegar
- Salt and pepper, to taste

Preparation

1. Take a Ziploc bag and add all Ingredients into it.

2. Marinate for at least 2 hours in your refrigerator.

3. Insert the crisper basket, and close the hood.

4. Pre-heat Ninja Foodi by squeezing the "AIR CRISP" alternative at 390 degrees F for 40 minutes.

5. Place the grill pan accessory in the Grill.

6. Flip the chicken after every 10 minutes.

7. Take a saucepan and pour the marinade into it and heat over medium flame until sauce thickens.

8. Brush with the glaze.

Serving Suggestion: Serve warm and enjoy.

Variation Tip: use salt and pepper instead of BBQ sauce for variation.

Nutritional Information per Serving:

Calories: 460| Fat: 20 g| Carbohydrates: 26 g| Fiber: 3 g| Sodium: 126 mg| Protein: 28 g

Alfredo Chicken Apples

Prep Time: 5-10 minutes

Cook Time: 20 minutes

Servings: 4

Ingredients

- 1 large apple, wedged
- 1 tablespoon lemon juice
- 4 chicken breasts, halved
- 4 tsp chicken seasoning

- 4 slices provolone cheese
- ¼ cup blue cheese, crumbled
- ½ cup Alfredo sauce

Preparation

1. Take a bowl and add chicken, season it well.

2. Take another bowl and add in apple, lemon juice.

3. Pre-heat Ninja Foodi by pressing the "GRILL" option and setting it to "MED" and timer to 20 minutes.

4. Let it pre-heat until you hear a beep.

5. Arrange chicken over Grill Grate, lock lid and cook for 8 minutes, flip and cook for 8 minutes more.

6. Grill apple in the same manner for 2 minutes per side.

Serving Suggestion: Serve chicken with pepper, apple, blue cheese, and Alfredo sauce and Enjoy!

Variation Tip: use pears for variations.

Nutritional Information per Serving:

Calories: 247|Fat: 19 g| Carbohydrates: 29 g| Fiber: 6 g |Sodium: 853 mg| Protein: 14 g

The Tarragon Chicken Meal

Prep Time: 10 minutes

Cook Time: 5 minutes

Servings: 4

Ingredients

For Chicken

- 1 and ½ pounds chicken tenders
- Salt as needed
- 3 tbsp tarragon leaves, chopped
- 1 tsp lemon zest, grated
- 2 tbsp fresh lemon juice
- 2 tbsp extra virgin olive oil

For Sauce

- 2 tbsp fresh lemon juice
- 2 tbsp butter, salted
- ½ cup heavy whip cream

Preparation

1. Prepare your chicken by taking a baking dish and arranging the chicken over the dish in a single layer.

2. Season generously with salt and pepper.

3. Sprinkle chopped tarragon and lemon zest all around the tenders.

4. Drizzle lemon juice and olive oil on top.

5. Let them sit for 10 minutes.

6. Drain them well.

7. Insert Grill Grate in your Ninja Foodi Grill and set to HIGH temperature.

8. Set timer to 4 minutes.

9. Once you hear the beep, place chicken tenders in your grill grate.

10. Let it cook for 3-4 minutes until cooked completely.

11. Do in batches if needed.

12. Transfer the cooked chicken tenders to a platter.

13. For the sauce, take a small-sized saucepan.

14. Add cream, butter and lemon juice and bring to a boil.

15. Once thickened enough, pour the mix over chicken.

16. Serve and enjoy!

Serving Suggestion: Serve with pita bread.

Variation Tip: use chopped dill for garnish.

Nutritional Information per Serving:

Calories: 263|Fat: 18 g| Carbohydrates: 7 g| Fiber: 1 g| Sodium: 363 mg| Protein: 19 g

Hearty Chicken Zucchini Kabobs

Prep Time: 10 minutes

Cook Time: 15 minutes

Servings: 4

Ingredients

- 1-pound chicken breast, boneless, skinless and cut into cubes of 2 inches
- 2 tbsp Greek yogurt, plain
- 4 lemons juice
- 1 lemon zest
- ¼ cup extra-virgin olive oil
- 2 tbsp oregano
- 1 red onion, quartered
- 1 zucchini, sliced
- 4 garlic cloves, minced
- 1 tsp of sea salt
- ½ tsp ground black pepper

Preparation

1. Take a mixing bowl, add the Greek yogurt, lemon juice, oregano, garlic, zest, salt, and pepper, combine them well.

2. Add the chicken and coat well, refrigerate for 1-2 hours to marinate.

3. Arrange the grill grate and close the lid.

4. Pre-heat Ninja Foodi by pressing the "GRILL" option and setting it to "MED" and timer to 7 minutes.

5. Take the skewers, thread the chicken, zucchini and red onion and thread alternatively.

6. Let it pre-heat until you hear a beep.

7. Arrange the skewers over the grill grate lock lid and cook until the timer reads zero.

8. Baste the kebabs with a marinating mixture in between.

9. Take out your when it reaches 165 degrees F.

10. Serve warm and enjoy.

Serving Suggestion: Serve with ranch sauce.

Variation Tip: use tomatoes with zucchini.

Nutritional Information per Serving:

Calories: 277| Fat: 15 g| Carbohydrates: 10 g| Fiber: 2 g| Sodium: 146 mg

Daisy Fresh Maple Chicken

Prep Time: 10 minutes

Cook Time: 15 minutes

Servings: 4

Ingredients

- 2 tsp onion powder
- 2 tsp garlic powder
- 3 garlic cloves, minced
- ⅓ cup soy sauce
- 1 cup maple syrup
- ¼ cup teriyaki sauce
- 1 tsp black pepper
- 2 pounds chicken wings, bone-in

Preparation

1. Take a medium-sized bowl and add soy sauce, garlic, pepper, maple syrup, garlic powder, onion powder, teriyaki sauce and mix well

2. Add the chicken wings to the mixture and coat it gently

3. Preheat your Ninja Foodi Grill in MED mode, setting the timer to 10 minutes

4. Once you hear a beep, arrange your prepared wings in the grill grate

5. Cook for 5 minutes, flip and cook for 5 minutes more until the internal temperature reaches 165 degrees F

Serving Suggestion: Serve with chilled red wine.

Variation Tip: sprinkle chopped dill for freshness.

Nutritional Information per Serving:

Calories: 543| Fat: 26 g| Carbohydrates: 46 g| Fiber: 4 g| Sodium: 648 mg| Protein: 42 g

Chicken Chili and Beans

Prep Time: 10 minutes

Cook Time: 15 minutes

Servings: 4

Ingredients

- 1 and ¼ pounds chicken breast, cut into pieces
- 1 can corn
- ¼ tsp garlic powder
- 1 can black beans, drained and rinsed
- 1 tablespoon oil
- 2 tbsp chili powder
- 1 bell pepper, chopped
- ¼ tsp garlic powder
- ¼ tsp salt

Preparation

1. Pre-heat Ninja Foodi by squeezing the "AIR CRISP" alternative and setting it to "360 Degrees F" and timer to 15 minutes.

2. Place all the Ingredients in your Ninja Foodi Grill cooking basket/alternatively, you may use a dish to mix the Ingredients and then put the dish in the cooking basket.

3. Stir to mix well.

4. Cook for 15 minutes.

5. Serve and enjoy!

Serving Suggestion: Serve warm and enjoy.

Variation Tip: add mushroom for freshness.

Nutritional Information per Serving:

Calories: 220| Fat: 4 g| Carbohydrates: 24 g| Fiber: 2 g| Sodium: 856 mg | Protein: 20 g

Classic BBQ Chicken Delight

Prep Time: 5-10 minutes

Cook Time: 12 minutes

Servings: 4

Ingredients:

- ⅓ cup spice seasoning
- ½ tablespoon Worcestershire sauce
- 1 tsp dried onion, chopped
- 1 tablespoon bourbon
- 1 tablespoon brown sugar
- ½ cup ketchup
- 1 pinch salt

- 2 tsp BBQ seasoning
- 6 chicken drumsticks

Preparation:

1. Take your saucepan and add listed Ingredients except for drumsticks, stir cook for 8-10 minutes

2. Keep it on the side and let them cool

3. Pre-heat your Ninja Foodi Grill to MED and set the timer to 12 minutes

4. Once the beep sound is heard, arrange your drumsticks over the grill grate and brush with remaining sauce

5. Cook for 6 minutes, flip with some more sauce and grill for 6 minutes more

6. Enjoy once done!

Serving Suggestion: Serve with sauce and enjoy.

Variation Tip: use pepper flakes for spiciness.

Nutritional Information per Serving:

Calories: 300| Fat: 8 g| Carbohydrates: 10 g | Fiber: 1.5 g |Sodium: 319 mg| Protein: 12.5 g

Delicious Maple Glazed Chicken

Prep Time: 10 minutes

Cook Time: 15 minutes

Servings: 4

Ingredients

- 2 pounds chicken wings, bone-in
- 1 tsp black pepper, ground
- ¼ cup teriyaki sauce
- 1 cup maple syrup
- ⅓ cup soy sauce
- 3 garlic cloves, minced
- 2 tsp garlic powder
- 2 tsp onion powder

Preparation

1. Take a mixing bowl, add garlic, soy sauce, black pepper, maple syrup, garlic powder, onion powder, and teriyaki sauce, combine well.

2. Add the chicken wings and combine well to coat.

3. Arrange the grill grate and close the lid.

4. Pre-heat Ninja Foodi by pressing the "GRILL" option and setting it to "MED" and timer to 10 minutes.

5. Let it pre-heat until you hear a beep.

6. Arrange the chicken wings over the grill grate lock lid and cook for 5 minutes.

7. Flip the chicken and close the lid, cook for 5 minutes more.

8. Cook until it reaches 165 degrees F.

9. Serve warm and enjoy!

Serving Suggestion: Serve with chilled wine.

Variation Tip: add pepper flakes for more spice.

Nutritional Information Per Serving:

Calories: 543| Fat: 26 g| Carbohydrates: 46 g| Fiber: 4 g| Sodium: 648 mg | Protein: 42 g

BBQ Chicken Drumstick

Prep Time: 5-10 minutes

Cook Time: 12 minutes

Servings: 5

Ingredients

- ⅓ cup spice seasoning
- ½ tablespoon Worcestershire sauce
- 1 tsp dried onion, chopped
- 1 tablespoon bourbon
- 1 tablespoon brown sugar
- ½ cup ketchup
- 1 pinch salt
- 2 tsp seasoned BBQ
- 6 chicken drumsticks

Preparation

1. Take a deep pan and add all Ingredients except for drumsticks, stir the mixture well.

2. Place it over medium heat, and stir cook for 8-10 minutes.

3. Keep the mix on the side.

4. Pre-heat your Ninja Foodi Grill to "MED" mode and set the timer to 12 minutes.

5. Once you hear beep arranges the drumsticks over grill grate and brush half of your prepared sauce.

6. Cook for 6 minutes, flip and brush more sauce, cook for 6 minutes more.

Serving Suggestion: Serve and enjoy once done with any remaining sauce.

Variation Tip: use turkey drumsticks for taste.

Nutritional Information per Serving:

Calories: 342|Fat: 9 g| Carbohydrates: 10 g| Fiber: 2 g| Sodium: 319 mg| Protein: 12 g

Baked Coconut Chicken

Prep Time: 10 minutes

Cook Time: 12 minutes

Servings: 4

Ingredients

- 2 large eggs
- 2 tsp garlic powder
- 1 tsp salt
- ½ tsp ground black pepper
- ¾ cup coconut aminos
- 1-pound chicken tenders
- Cooking spray as needed

Preparation

1. Pre-heat Ninja Foodi by squeezing the "AIR CRISP" alternative and setting it to "400 Degrees F" and timer to 12 minutes.

2. Take a large-sized baking sheet and spray it with cooking spray.

3. Take a wide dish and add garlic powder, eggs, pepper, and salt.

4. Whisk well until everything is combined.

5. Add the almond meal and coconut and mix well.

6. Take your chicken tenders and dip them in the egg followed by dipping in the coconut mix.

7. Shake off any excess.

8. Transfer them to your Ninja Foodi Grill and spray the tenders with a bit of oil.

9. Cook for 12-14 minutes until you have a nice golden-brown texture.

Serving Suggestion: Serve warm.

Variation Tip: use almond for crunch.

Nutritional Information Per Serving:

Calories: 180| Fat: 1 g| Carbohydrates: 3 g| Fiber: 1 g| Sodium: 214 mg| Protein: 0 g

Grilled Orange Chicken

Prep Time: 5-10 minutes

Cook Time: 10 minutes

Servings: 5-6

Ingredients

- 2 tsp ground coriander
- ½tsp garlic salt
- ¼ tsp ground black pepper
- 12 chicken wings
- 1 tablespoon canola oil

Sauce

- ¼ cup butter, melted
- 3 tbsp honey
- ½ cup orange juice
- ⅓ cup Sriracha chili sauce
- 2 tbsp lime juice
- ¼ cup chopped cilantro

Preparation

1. Coat chicken with oil and season with the spices; refrigerate for 2 hours to marinate.

2. Combine all the sauce Ingredients and set aside. Optionally, you can stir-cook the sauce mixture for 3-4 minutes in a saucepan.

3. Take Ninja Foodi Grill, organize it over your kitchen stage, and open the top cover.

4. Organize the barbecue mesh and close the top cover.

5. Click "GRILL" and choose the "MED" grill function. Adjust the timer to 10 minutes and afterward press "START/STOP." Ninja Foodi will begin pre-warming.

6. Ninja Foodi is preheated and prepared to cook when it begins to signal. After you hear a blare, open the top.

7. Organize chicken over the grill grate.

8. Close the top lid and cook for 5 minutes. Now open the top lid, flip the chicken.

9. Close the top lid and cook for 5 more minutes.

Serving Suggestion: Serve with fresh salad.

Variation Tip: add vinegar instead of lime juice.

Nutritional Information Per Serving:

Calories: 327| Fat: 14g| Carbohydrates: 19g| Fiber: 1g| Sodium: 258mg| Protein: 25g

Orange Grilled Chicken Meal

Prep Time: 5-10 minutes

Cook Time: 15 minutes

Servings: 4

Ingredients:

- 12 chicken wings
- 2 tbsp lime juice
- ¼ cup cilantro, chopped
- 2 tsp coriander, grounded
- 1 tablespoon canola oil
- ⅓ cup Sriracha chili sauce
- ¼ cup butter, melted
- 3 tbsp honey
- ½ cup of orange juice
- ½ tsp garlic salt
- ¼ tsp ground black pepper

Preparation:

1. Coat the chicken with oil, season with spices.

2. Let it chill for 2 hours.

3. Add listed Ingredients and keep it on the side.

4. Cook for 3-4 minutes in a saucepan.

5. Pre-heat your Ninja Foodi by pressing the "GRILL" option and setting it to "MED."

6. Set your timer to 10 minutes.

7. Let it pre-heat until it beeps.

8. Arrange chicken over grill grate, cook for 5 minutes.

9. Flip and let it cook for 5 minutes more.

10. Serve and enjoy!

Serving Suggestion: Serve with sauce on top.

Variation Tip: use lean beef for unique taste.

Nutritional Information per Serving:

Calories: 320| Fat: 14 g| Carbohydrates: 19 g| Fiber: 1 g| Sodium: 258 mg| Protein: 25 g

JUICY BEEF, LAMB AND PORK

Chipotle-Raspberry Pork Chops

Prep Time: 10 minutes

Cook Time: 10 minutes

Servings: 4

Ingredients

- ½ cup seedless raspberry
- 4 bone-in pork loin chops (7 ounces each)
- 1 chipotle pepper in adobo sauce, finely chopped
- ½ tsp salt

Preparation

1. Preheat the grill for five minutes.

2. In a saucepan, cook and stir and chipotle pepper over medium heat until heated through. Reserve 1/4 cup for serving. Sprinkle pork with salt; brush with remaining raspberry sauce.

3. Lightly grease a grill or broiler pan rack. Set the temperature to MAX, and set time to five minutes. Select the option START/STOP to begin preheating.

Serving Suggestion: Serve with raspberry sauce.

Variation Tip: for spice add pepper to your taste.

Nutritional Information Per Serving:

Calories 412 | Carbohydrates 64.3g | Protein 16.1g | Fat 10.1g | Sodium 895mg| Fiber 2g

Delicious Pot Roast

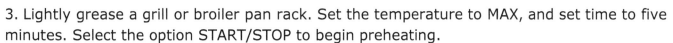

Prep Time: 10 minutes.

Cook Time: 6 hours.

Serves: 6

Ingredients

Seasoning Blend

- 2 tsp thyme leaves dried
- 2 tsp sea salt
- 1 tsp black pepper
- 1 tsp garlic powder
- 1 tsp onion powder
- ½ tsp red pepper flakes

Pot Roast Ingredients

- 1-2 Tbsp avocado oil
- 3-41 bs Chuck Roast
- 1 onion

- 4 cups beef stock divided
- ¼ cup flour
- 6 carrots
- 6 small potatoes

Preparation

1. Add the oil to the inner pan of the indoor Grill and preheat on high grill (500°F/260°C).
2. Combine the seasoning in a bowl and rub onto both sides of the chuck roast. When the grill has preheated, place the roast on the bottom of the inner pan. Close the lid and grill on high for 5 minutes.
3. Flip and grill another 5 minutes.
4. Cut your onion into chunks and add to the pan. Pour in 2 cups of beef stock and select the Roast function on 250°F/121°C and set the time for 3 hours.
5. After the 3 hours, remove the meat and make the gravy by combining the remaining beef stock and flour with some of the liquid in the pan into a large glass Mason jar with a lid and shake until well combined.
6. Pour into the pan. Put the roast in along with the vegetables and set the grill to the roast setting on 250°F/121°C for another 3 hours.
7. The total cook time will depend on your roast, so start checking it after the 1st hour and give it a flip.

Serving Suggestion: Serve with the vegetables.

Variation Tip: For keto version uses ½ cup of coconut flour for gravy.

Nutritional Information Per Serving:

Calories 658 | Carbohydrates 44g | Protein 52g | Fat 31g | Sodium 156mg| Fiber 6g

Steak Pineapple Mania

Prep Time: 5-10 minutes

Cook Time: 8 minutes

Servings: 4-5

Ingredients

- ½ medium pineapple, cored and diced
- 1 jalapeño pepper, seeded, stemmed, and diced
- 1 medium red onion, diced
- 4 (6-8-ounce) filet mignon steaks
- 1 tablespoon canola oil
- Sea salt and ground black pepper to taste
- 1 tablespoon lime juice
- ¼ cup chopped cilantro leaves
- Chili powder and ground coriander to taste

Preparation

1. Rub the fillets with the oil evenly, and then season with the salt and black pepper.
2. Take Ninja Foodi Grill, arrange it over your kitchen platform, and open the top lid.

3. Arrange the grill grate and close the top lid.

4. Press "GRILL" and select the "HIGH" grill function. Adjust the timer to 8 minutes and then press "START/STOP." Ninja Foodi will start preheating.

5. Ninja Foodi is preheated and ready to cook when it starts to beep. After you hear a beep, open the top lid.

6. Arrange the fillets over the grill grate. Close the top lid and cook for 4 minutes. Now open the top lid, flip the fillets.

7. Close the top lid and cook for 4 more minutes. Cook until the food thermometer reaches 125°F.

8. In a mixing bowl, add the pineapple, onion, and jalapeño. Combine well. Add the lime juice, cilantro, chili powder, and coriander. Combine again.

Serving Suggestion: Serve the fillets warm with the pineapple mixture on top.

Variation Tip: Add chilies for spicy taste.

Nutritional Information Per Serving:
Calories: 536| Fat: 22.5g|Carbohydrates: 21g| Fiber: 4g|Sodium: 286mg|Protein: 58g

Grilled Beef Burgers

Prep Time: 5-10 minutes

Cook Time: 10 minutes

Servings: 4

Ingredients

- 4 pounces cream cheese
- 4 slices bacon, cooked and crumbled
- 2 seeded jalapeño peppers, stemmed, and minced
- ½ cup shredded Cheddar cheese
- ½ tsp chili powder
- ¼ tsp paprika
- ¼ tsp ground black pepper
- 2 pounds ground beef
- 4 hamburger buns
- 4 slices pepper Jack cheese
- Optional - Lettuce, sliced tomato, and sliced red onion

Preparation

1. In a mixing bowl, combine the peppers, Cheddar cheese, cream cheese, and bacon until well combined.

2. Prepare the ground beef into 8 patties. Add the cheese mixture onto four of the patties; arrange a second patty on top of each to prepare four burgers. Press gently.

3. In another bowl, combine the chili powder, paprika, and pepper. Sprinkle the mixture onto the sides of the burgers.

4. Take Ninja Foodi Grill, organize it over your kitchen stage, and open the top cover.

5. Organize the flame broil mesh and close the top cover.

6. Press "Flame broil" and select the "HIGH" barbecue work. Change the clock to 4 minutes and afterward press "START/STOP." Ninja Foodi will begin pre-warming.

7. Ninja Foodi is preheated and prepared to cook when it begins to blare. After you hear a blare, open the top. Arrange the burgers over the grill grate.

8. Close the top lid and allow it to cook until the timer reads zero. Cook for 3-4 more minutes, if needed.

9. Cook until the food thermometer reaches 145°F. Serve warm.

Serving Suggestion: Serve warm with buns.

Variation Tip: Add your choice of toppings: pepper Jack cheese, lettuce, tomato, and red onion.

Nutritional Information Per Serving:

Calories: 783| Fat: 38g| Carbohydrates: 25g| Fiber: 3g| Sodium: 1259mg| Protein: 57.5g

Bourbon Pork Chops

Prep Time: 5-10 minutes

Cook Time: 20 minutes

Servings: 4

Ingredients

- 4 boneless pork chops
- Ocean salt and ground dark pepper to taste
- ¼ cup apple cider vinegar
- ¼ cup soy sauce
- 3 tbsp Worcestershire sauce
- 2 cups ketchup
- ¾ cup bourbon
- 1 cup packed brown sugar
- ½ tablespoon dry mustard powder

Preparation

1. Take Ninja Foodi Grill, orchestrate it over your kitchen stage, and open the top cover. Orchestrate the flame broil mesh and close the top cover.

2. Click "GRILL" and choose the "MED" grill function. Adjust the timer to 15 minutes and click "START/STOP."

3. Ninja Foodi is preheated and prepared to cook when it begins to signal. After you hear a signal, open the top.

4. Arrange the pork chops over the grill grate.

5. Close the top lid and cook for 8 minutes. Now open the top lid, flip the pork chops.

6. Close the top lid and cook for 8 more minutes. Check the pork chops for doneness, cook for 2 more minutes if required.

7. In a saucepan, heat the soy sauce, sugar, ketchup, bourbon, vinegar, Worcestershire sauce, and mustard powder; stir-cook until boils.

8. Reduce heat and simmer for 20 minutes to thicken the sauce.

9. Coat the pork chops with salt and ground black pepper.

Serving Suggestion: Serve warm with the prepared sauce.

Variation Tip: use beef for variation.

Nutritional Information per Serving:

Calories: 346| Fat: 13.5g| Carbohydrates: 27g| Fiber: 0.5g|Sodium: 1324mg|Protein: 27g

Spinach Salad with Steak & Blueberries

Prep Time: 30 minutes

Cook Time: 30 minutes

Servings: 4

Ingredients

- 1 cup fresh blueberries, divided
- ½ cup chopped walnuts, toasted
- 1 tsp sugar
- ½ tsp salt, divided
- 3 tbsp fruity vinegar, such as raspberry vinegar
- 1 tablespoon minced shallot
- 3 tbsp walnut oil or canola oil
- 8 cups baby spinach
- 1 pound sirloin steak
- ½ tsp freshly ground pepper
- ¼ cup crumbled feta cheese

Preparation

1. Preheat the grill for eight minutes.

2. Pulse quarter cup blueberries, quarter cup walnuts, vinegar, shallots, ¼ tsp salt, and sugar in a food processor to form a paste. With the running motor, add oil until incorporated. Then transfer the dressing to a big bowl.

3. Sprinkle the steak with pepper and the left quarter with tsp salt.

4. Insert grill grate in the unit and close the hood. Select the option GRILL, set the temperature to MAX, and set time to six minutes. Select the option START/STOP to begin preheating.

5. Add the spinach to a bowl with the dressing and toss to coat. Divide the spinach among four plates. Slice the steak thinly, crosswise.

Serving Suggestion: Serve top spinach with the feta, steak, and remaining blueberries and walnuts.

Variation Tip: use fresh berries of your choice.

Nutritional Information per Serving:

Calories 412 | Carbohydrates 64.3g | Protein 16.1g | Fat 10.1g | Sodium 895mg| Fiber 2g

Grilled Pork Tenderloin Marinated in Spicy Soy Sauce

Prep Time: 20 minutes

Cook Time: 140 minutes

Servings: 6

Ingredients

- ¼ cup reduced-sodium soy sauce
- 1 tablespoon finely grated fresh ginger
- 2 tbsp sugar
- 1 large garlic clove, minced
- 1 fresh red Thai chile, minced
- 1 tablespoon toasted sesame oil
- 1½ pounds pork tenderloin, trimmed of fat and cut into 1-inch-thick medallions

Preparation

1. Preheat the grill for eight minutes.

2. Whisk the soy sauce and sugar in a medium bowl until the sugar is dissolved. Stir in ginger, garlic, chili, and oil.

3. Place the pork in a plastic bag. Add the marinade and then seal the bag, squeezing out the air. Turn the bag for coating the medallions. Refrigerate for two hours, turning bag once to redistribute the marinade.

4. Insert grill grate in the unit and close the hood. Remove the pork. Select the option GRILL, set the temperature to MED, and set time to six minutes. Select the option START/STOP to begin preheating.

Serving Suggestion: Serve hot with cold wine.

Variation Tip: use cayenne Chile pepper for spice.

Nutritional Information Per Serving:

Calories 155.5 | Carbohydrates 24.8g | Protein 3g | Fat 5.4g | Sodium 193.7mg| Fiber 1 g

Lettuce Cheese Steak

Prep Time: 5-10 minutes

Cook Time: 16 minutes

Servings: 5-6

Ingredients

- 4 (8-ounce) skirt steaks
- 6 cups romaine lettuce, chopped
- ¾ cup cherry tomatoes halved
- ¼ cup blue cheese, crumbled
- Ocean salt and Ground Black Pepper

- 2 avocados, peeled and sliced
- 1 cup croutons
- 1 cup blue cheese dressing

Preparation

1. Coat steaks with black pepper and salt.

2. Take Ninja Foodi Grill, mastermind it over your kitchen stage, and open the top. Organize the barbecue mesh and close the top.

3. Click "GRILL" and choose the "HIGH" function. Change the clock to 8 minutes and afterward press "START/STOP." Ninja Foodi will begin pre-warming.

4. Ninja Foodi is preheated and prepared to cook when it begins to blare. After you hear a blare, open the top cover.

5. Fix finely the 2 steaks on the barbeque mesh.

6. Close the top cover and cook for 4 minutes. Presently open the top cover, flip the steaks.

7. Close the top cover and cook for 4 additional minutes. Cook until the food thermometer comes to 165°F. Cook for 3-4 more minutes if needed. Grill the remaining steaks.

8. In a mixing bowl, add the lettuce, tomatoes, blue cheese, and croutons. Combine the Ingredients to mix well with each other.

Serving Suggestion: Serve the steaks warm with the salad mixture, blue cheese dressing, and avocado slices on top.

Variation Tip: use your favorite steak

Nutritional Information per Serving:

Calories: 576|, Fat: 21g| Carbohydrates: 23g| Fiber: 6.5g|Sodium: 957mg|Protein: 53.5g

Turmeric Pork Chops with Green Onion Rice

Prep Time: 15 minutes

Cook Time: 15 minutes

Servings: 4

Ingredients

- 4 (6-oz.) bone-in pork chops
- ½ tsp kosher salt, divided
- ½ tsp black pepper, divided
- 3 tbsp olive oil, divided
- 1 large garlic clove, halved
- ½ tsp ground turmeric
- 1 tablespoon fish sauce
- 2 tsp oyster sauce
- 1 tsp tomato paste

- 1 bunch green onions
- 2 (8.8-oz.) packages precooked brown rice
- ¼ cup fresh cilantro leaves
- 1 lime, cut into 4 wedges

Preparation

1. Heat the grill for 8 minutes before use. Rub pork with cut sides of garlic; discard garlic. Sprinkle pork with turmeric, ¼ tsp salt, and ¼ tsp pepper. Combine 2 tsp oil, fish sauce, oyster sauce, and tomato paste.

2. Brush both sides of pork with half of the oil mixture. Grill pork for 4 minutes on each side or until the desired degree of doneness. Transfer to a plate; brush both sides of pork with the remaining oil mixture. Keep warm.

3. Add onions to grill. Over medium-high; grill for 2 minutes. Coarsely chop onions.

4. Heat rice according to package Preparation. Combine green onions, rice, remaining one tablespoon oil, ¼ tsp salt, and ¼ tsp pepper.

Serving Suggestion: Serve rice with pork. Sprinkle with cilantro; serve with lime wedges.

Variation Tip: can be eat without rice and taste will be marvelous.

Nutritional Information Per Serving:

Calories 412 | Carbohydrates 64.3g | Protein 16.1g | Fat 10.1g | Sodium 895mg| Fiber 2g

Avocado Salsa Steak

Prep Time: 5-10 minutes

Cook Time: 18 minutes

Servings: 4

Ingredients

- 1 cup cilantro leaves
- 2 ripe avocados, diced
- 2 cups salsa Verde
- 2 beef flank steak, diced
- ½ tsp salt
- ½ tsp pepper
- 2 medium tomatoes, seeded and diced

Preparation

1. Rub the beef steak with salt and black pepper to season well.

2. Take Ninja Foodi Grill, orchestrate it over your kitchen stage, and open the top cover.

3. Orchestrate the flame broil mesh and close the top cover.

4. Press "Barbecue" and select the "MED" flame broil work. Alter the clock to 18 minutes and afterward press "START/STOP." Ninja Foodi will begin pre-warming.

5. Ninja Foodi is preheated and prepared to cook when it begins to signal. After you hear a blare, open the top. Arrange the diced steak over the grill grate.

6. Close the top lid and cook for 9 minutes. Now open the top lid, flip the diced steak.

7. Close the top lid and cook for 9 more minutes.

8. In a blender, blend the salsa and cilantro.

Serving Suggestion: Serve the grilled steak with the blended salsa, tomato, and avocado.

Variation Tip: for spicier steak use cayenne pepper.

Nutritional Information Per Serving:

Calories: 523| Fat: 31.5g|Carbohydrates: 38.5g| Fiber: 2g| Sodium: 301mg| Protein: 41.5g

Sausage and Pepper Grinders

Prep Time: 15 minutes

Cook Time: 26 minutes

Servings: 6

Ingredients

• 2 bell peppers, cut in quarters, seeds and ribs removed

• Kosher salt, as desired

• Ground black pepper, as desired

• 1 white onion, peeled, sliced in 1-inch rings

• 2 tbsp canola oil, divided

• 6 raw sausages (4 ounces each)

• 6 hot dog buns

• Condiments, as desired

Preparation

1. Preheat for eight minutes.

2. Insert grill grate in the unit and close the hood. Select the option GRILL, set the temperature to LOW, and set time to twenty-six minutes. Select the option START/STOP to begin preheating.

3. When the unit starts beeping to signal that it has preheated, place steaks on the grill grate. Close hood and cook for 12 minutes.

4. After twelve minutes, transfer the peppers and onions to a medium mixing bowl. Place the sausages on the grill grate; close the hood and cook for 6 minutes.

5. After six minutes, flip the sausages. Close the hood and cook for six extra minutes.

6. Meanwhile, gently tear up the grilled onions into individual rings and mix them well with the peppers.

7. After six minutes, remove the sausages from the grill grate. Place the buns, cut-side them down, over the grill grate. Close the hood and cook for 2 remaining minutes.

8. When cooking is done, spread any desired condiments on the buns, then place the sausages in buns.

Serving Suggestion: Serve topped each with onions peppers.

Variation Tip: use your preferred condiments.

Nutritional Information Per Serving:

Calories 155.5 | Carbohydrates 24.8g | Protein 3g | Fat 5.4g | Sodium 193.7mg| Fiber 1g

Korean Chili Pork

Prep Time: 5-10 minutes

Cook Time: 8 minutes

Servings: 4

Ingredients

- 2 pounds pork, cut into ⅛-inch slices
- 5 minced garlic cloves
- 3 tbsp minced green onion
- 1 yellow onion, sliced
- ½ cup soy sauce
- ½ cup brown sugar
- 3 tbsp regular chili paste
- 2 tbsp sesame seeds
- 3 tsp black pepper
- Red pepper flakes to taste

Preparation

1. Take a zip-lock bag, add all the Ingredients. Shake well and refrigerate for 6-8 hours to marinate.

2. Take Ninja Foodi Grill, orchestrate it over your kitchen stage, and open the top.

3. Mastermind the barbecue mesh and close the top cover.

4. Click "GRILL" and choose the "MED" grill function. flame broil work. Modify the clock to 8 minutes and afterward press "START/STOP." Ninja Foodi will begin to warm up.

5. Ninja Foodi is preheated and prepared to cook when it begins to signal. After you hear a signal, open the top.

6. Fix finely sliced pork on the barbeque mesh.

7. Cover and cook for 4 minutes. Then open the cover, switch the side of the pork.

8. Cover it and cook for another 4 minutes.

Serving Suggestion: Serve warm with chopped lettuce.

Variation Tip: for spiciness use Korean red chili paste.

Nutritional Information Per Serving:

Calories: 621| Fat: 31g|Carbohydrates: 29g|Fiber: 3g| Sodium: 1428mg| Protein: 53g

Grilled Steak Salad with Tomatoes & Eggplant

Prep Time: 40 minutes

Cook Time: 40 minutes

Servings: 4

Ingredients

- 1 tablespoon dried oregano
- 1pound flank steak, trimmed
- 1 small eggplant cut lengthwise into ½-inch-thick slices
- 4 tbsp extra-virgin olive oil, divided
- 1 tsp salt, divided
- ¾ tsp freshly ground pepper, divided
- 2 sweet Italian peppers, cut into 2-inch-wide strips
- 2 large tomatoes, cut into wedges
- 1 small red onion, thinly sliced
- 1 small clove garlic, minced
- 3 tbsp red-wine vinegar

Preparation

1. Preheat the grill for eight minutes.

2. Cook the oregano in a small skillet on medium heat and keep stirring until it is toasted, which will be about two minutes. Transfer it to a bowl.

3. Cut the steak in half, lengthwise; season it with half tsp each salt and pepper. Brush the peppers and eggplant with one tablespoon oil.

4. Insert grill grate in the unit and close the hood. Select the option GRILL, set the temperature to LOW, and set time to thirty minutes. Select the option START/STOP to begin preheating.

5. Add the tomatoes, garlic, and onion to a bowl with the oregano. Drizzle them with vinegar and the remaining 3 tsp oil. Season them with the remaining half tsp salt and quarter tsp pepper; toss to combine. Chop the eggplant and peppers and cut the steak across the grain into thin slices; add to the bowl and toss to combine.

Serving Suggestion: Serve warm.

Variation Tip: add your favorite veggies for the salad.

Nutritional Information Per Serving:

Calories 177.6 | Carbohydrates 25.5g | Protein 5 g | Fat 8.9g | Sodium 286.5mg| Fiber 2.5g

CRISPY FISH AND SEAFOOD

Grilled Salmon Packets

Prep Time: 5 minutes

Cook Time: 15-20 minutes

Servings: 4

Ingredients

- 4 salmon steaks (6 ounces each)
- 1 tsp lemon-pepper seasoning
- 1 cup shredded carrots
- 1 tsp dried parsley flakes
- ½ cup julienned sweet yellow pepper
- ½ cup julienned green pepper
- 4 tsp lemon juice
- ½ tsp salt
- 1/4 tsp pepper

Preparation

1. Preheat the grill for five minutes.

2. Sprinkle the salmon with a lemon-pepper. Place each of the salmon steaks on a double thickness of heavy-duty foil (about 12 in. square). Top with carrots and peppers. Sprinkle with remaining Ingredients.

3. Fold foil around fish and seal them tightly. Then Grill, covered, over medium heat for 15-20 minutes or until fish flakes easily with a fork.

Serving Suggestion: Serve with dill garnishing or enjoy as it is.

Variation Tip: use chopped dill for garnish.

Nutritional Information Per Serving:

Calories 98 | Carbohydrates 7.1g | Protein 1.3g | Fat 6.5g | Sodium 154.6mg| Fiber 0g

Grilled Lemon-Garlic Salmon

Prep Time: 10 minutes

Cook Time: 15-20 minutes

Servings: 4

Ingredients

- 2 garlic cloves, minced
- ½ tsp minced fresh rosemary
- 2 tsp grated lemon zest
- ½ tsp salt
- ½ tsp pepper
- 4 salmon fillets (6 ounces each)

Preparation

1. Take a small bowl, mix the first five Ingredients, and rub over fillets. Let it stand for 15 minutes. Coat the grill with cooking oil.

2. Preheat the grill for 8 minutes before use. Place salmon on the grill with the skin side up. Grill while covered over medium heat or broil 4 in. From heat 4 minutes. Turn and grill 3 to 6 minutes longer or until fish just begins to flake easily with a fork.

Serving Suggestion: Serve with lemon wedges.

Variation Tip: use chopped dill for garnish.

Nutritional Information Per Serving:

Calories 280 | Carbohydrates 40g | Protein 4g | Fat 12g | Sodium 200mg| Fiber 1g

Apricot-Chile Glazed Salmon

Prep Time: 25 minutes

Cook Time: 25 minutes

Servings: 4

Ingredients

- 2 tbsp red chili powder
- 3 tbsp apricot jam
- ½ tsp salt
- 1¼-1½ pounds center-cut wild salmon, skinned

Preparation

1. Preheat the grill for eight minutes.

2. Combine the salt and chili powder in a bowl. Rub them onto both sides of salmon.

3. Place the jam in a saucepan; heat it over medium heat, keep stirring it until melted.

4. Insert grill grate in the unit and close the hood.

5. Select the option GRILL, set the temperature to MED, and set time to ten minutes. Select the option START/STOP to begin preheating. Use a pastry brush, coat the top of the salmon with the jam. Close the grill; cook until the salmon easily flakes with a fork, 3 to 5 minutes more. To serve, cut into 4 portions.

Serving Suggestion: Serve with chilled drink.

Variation Tip: use any jam of your liking for glaze.

Nutritional Information Per Serving:

Calories 151 | Carbohydrates 19.46g | Protein 1.85g | Fat 7.54g | Sodium 95mg| Fiber 0.4g

Grilled Salmon with Mustard & Herbs

Prep Time: 15 minutes

Cook Time: 40 minutes

Servings: 4

Ingredients

- 2 lemons, thinly sliced,
- 20-30 sprigs mixed fresh herbs, plus 2 tbsp chopped, divided
- 1 tablespoon Dijon mustard
- 1 pound center-cut salmon, skinned
- 1 clove garlic
- ¼ tsp salt

Preparation

1. Preheat the grill for eight minutes.

2. Lay the two nine-inch pieces of heavy-duty foil on top of one another and place it on a baking sheet. Arrange the lemon slices in two layers in the center of the foil. Spread the herb sprigs on the lemons. With the chef's knife, mash the garlic with salt and form a paste. Transfer it to a small dish and then stir in mustard and the remaining two tsp of chopped herbs. Spread the mixture on double sides of the salmon. Place the salmon on top of the herb sprigs.

3. Slide off the foil and salmon from the baking sheet onto the grill Insert grill grate in the unit and close the hood. Select the option GRILL, set the temperature to MAX, and set time to twenty-four minutes. Select the option START/STOP to begin preheating.

Serving Suggestion: Divide the salmon into four portions and serve it with lemon wedges.

Variation Tip: use chopped dill for garnish.

Nutritional Information Per Serving:

Calories 197.3 | Carbohydrates 21.5g | Protein 2.5g | Fat 11.6g | Sodium 59.8mg| Fiber 1 g

Grilled Salmon Soft Tacos

Prep Time: 20 minutes

Cook Time: 20 minutes

Servings: 4

Ingredients

- 2 tbsp extra-virgin olive oil
- 1 tablespoon ancho or New Mexico chile powder
- 4 4-ounce wild salmon fillets, about 1-inch thick, skin on
- 1 tablespoon fresh lime juice
- ¼ tsp kosher salt
- ⅛ tsp freshly ground pepper
- 8 6-inch corn or flour tortillas, warmed
- Cabbage Slaw
- Citrus Salsa
- Cilantro Crema

Preparation

1. Preheat the grill for eight minutes.

2. Combine chili powder, oil, lime juice, salt, and pepper in a bowl. Rub the spice mixture over salmon. Insert grill grate in the unit and close the hood. Select the option GRILL, set the temperature to LOW, and set time to eight minutes. Select the option START/STOP to begin preheating. Cut each of the fillets lengthwise into two pieces and then remove the skin.

Serving Suggestion: To serve, place two tortillas on each plate. Divide the fish, Citrus Salsa, Cabbage Slaw, and Cilantro Crema among the tortillas.

Variation Tip: use chopped dill for garnish.

Nutritional Information per Serving:

Calories 199.8 | Carbohydrates 25.6g | Protein 3.6g | Fat 2.2g | Sodium 147.6mg| Fiber 4.8g

Easy BBQ Roast Shrimp

Prep Time: 5-10 minutes

Cook Time: 7 minutes

Servings: 2

Ingredients

- ½ pound shrimps, large
- 3 tbsp chipotle in adobo sauce, minced
- ½ orange, juiced
- ¼ cup BBQ sauce
- ¼ tsp salt

Preparation

1. Add listed Ingredients into a mixing bowl.

2. Mix them well.

3. Keep it aside.

4. Pre-heat Ninja Foodi by pressing the "ROAST" option and setting it to "400 Degrees F.".

5. Set the timer to 7 minutes.

6. Let it pre-heat until you hear a beep.

7. Arrange shrimps over Grill Grate and lock lid.

8. cook for 7 minutes.

9. Serve and enjoy!

Serving Suggestion: Serve with dill garnishing.

Variation Tip: use chopped dill for garnish.

Nutritional Information Per Serving:

Calories: 173|Fat: 2 g| Carbohydrates: 21 g| Fiber: 2 g| Sodium: 1143 mg| Protein: 17 g

Paprika Grilled Shrimp

Prep Time: 5-10 minutes

Cook Time: 6 minutes

Servings: 4

Ingredients

- 1-pound jumbo shrimps, peeled and deveined
- 2 tbsp brown sugar
- 1 tablespoon paprika
- 1 tablespoon garlic powder
- 2 tbsp olive oil
- 1 tsp garlic salt
- ½ tsp black pepper

Preparation

1. Add listed Ingredients into a mixing bowl.

2. Mix them well.

3. Let it chill and marinate for 30-60 minutes.

4. Pre-heat Ninja Foodi by pressing the "GRILL" option and setting it to "MED.".

5. Set the timer to 6 minutes.

6. Let it pre-heat until you hear a beep.

7. Arrange prepared shrimps over the grill grate.

8. Lock lid and cook for 3 minutes.

9. Then flip and cook for 3 minutes more.

10. Serve and enjoy!

Serving Suggestion: Serve with dill garnishing or enjoy as it is.

Variation Tip: use hot chili powder for spicier.

Nutritional Information per Serving:

Calories: 370| Fat: 27 g| Carbohydrates: 23 g| Fiber: 8 g| Sodium: 182 mg| Protein: 6 g

Teriyaki-Marinated Salmon

Prep Time: 5 minutes

Cook Time: 8 minutes

Servings: 4

Ingredients

- 4 uncooked skinless salmon fillets (6 ounces each)
- 1 cup teriyaki marinade

Preparation

1. Put the fish fillets and teriyaki sauce in a big resalable plastic bag. Move the fillets around to coat everywhere with sauce. Refrigerate it for one to twelve hours as per your need.

2. Insert the grill grate in the unit and close the hood. Select the option GRILL, set the temperature to MAX, and set the time to eight minutes. Press START/STOP to begin preheating.

3. When the unit signals that it has preheated, put fillets on the grill, gently press them to maximize the grill marks. Close the hood and cook it for six minutes. There isn't a need to flip the fish while cooking.

4. After six minutes, check the fillets if done; the internal temperature should come at least 140°F. If necessary, close the hood and continue to cook for 2 more minutes.

5. After cooking, serve the fillets immediately.

Serving Suggestion: Serve with lemon wedges.

Variation Tip: use chopped dill for garnish.

Nutritional Information per Serving:

Calories 190 | Carbohydrates 26g | Protein 4g | Fat 9g | Sodium 105mg| Fiber 3g

Grilled Fish Tacos

Prep Time: 30 minutes

Cook Time: 50minutes

Servings: 6

Ingredients

- 4 tsp chili powder
- 2 tbsp lime juice
- 2 tbsp extra-virgin olive oil
- 1 tsp ground cumin
- 1 tsp onion powder
- 1 tsp garlic powder
- 1 tsp salt
- ½ tsp freshly ground pepper
- 2 pounds mahi-mahi, ¾ inch thick, skinned and cut into 4 portions
- ¼ cup reduced-fat sour cream
- ¼ cup low-fat mayonnaise
- 2 tbsp chopped fresh cilantro
- 1 tsp lime zest
- Freshly ground pepper
- 3 cups finely shredded red or green cabbage

- 2 tbsp lime juice
- 1 tsp sugar
- ⅛ tsp salt
- 12 corn tortillas, warmed

Preparation

1. To prepare the fish: Combine lime juice, chili powder, oil, cumin, onion powder, salt and pepper, garlic powder in a bowl. Rub the adobo over all the fish. Let it stand 20 to 30 minutes for the fish to absorb the flavor.

2. To prepare the coleslaw: Add lime juice, sour cream, mayonnaise, cilantro, lime zest, salt and pepper, sugar, in a medium bowl; mix them until smooth and creamy. Add the cabbage and toss it to combine. Refrigerate until ready to use.

3. Preheat the grill for eight minutes before use.

4. Insert grill grate in the unit and close the hood. Select the option GRILL, set the temperature to LOW, and set time to fifteen minutes. Select the option START/STOP to begin preheating.

5. Transfer the fish to a plate and then separate it into large chunks.

Serving Suggestion: Serve the tacos by passing the fish, tortillas, coleslaw and taco garnishes separately.

Variation Tip: use chopped dill for garnish.

Nutritional Information per Serving:

Calories 215.3 | Carbohydrates 19.4g | Protein 3.7g | Fat 14.7g | Sodium 83.8mg| Fiber 1.1g

Grilled Seafood Platter

Prep Time: 30 minutes

Cook Time: 10 minutes

Servings: 6

Ingredients

- 1 cup extra virgin olive oil
- 2 garlic cloves, finely chopped
- 2 tbsp chopped basil
- Zest and juice of 2 lemons
- 4 blue swimmer crabs, halved, claws cracked
- 4 lobster tails or small whole lobsters, halved, cleaned
- 24 scampi, peeled (tails intact), deveined
- 32 green prawns, peeled (tails intact), deveined
- 350g clams
- 12 scallops in the half shell
- 2 tbsp chopped flat-leaf parsley
- Avocado cream
- 2 ripe avocados, peeled, stoned, roughly chopped
- ½ cup thickened cream
- 1 garlic clove, chopped

- Juice of 1 lime

Seafood sauce

- 200ml whole-egg mayonnaise
- 1 small lime, zest grated, juiced
- 1 tbsp sweet chilli sauce
- 1 tbsp tomato sauce

Preparation

1. Combine the oil, garlic, basil, lemon juice and zest in a bowl, then season. Brush the marinade over the seafood.

2. Heat a ninja grill over medium-high. Cook the crab and lobster for 2 minutes, then add the scampi and cook for a further 2 minutes. Add the prawns and clams, and cook for 3-4 minutes, then add the scallops. When the clams open and the prawns and scallops are opaque, transfer all seafood to a platter. Serve with parsley, avocado and seafood sauces.

3. **To make the avocado cream**: Pulse ingredients in a food processor until smooth. Season to taste with sea salt and freshly ground black pepper.

4. **To make the seafood sauce**: Whisk the ingredients together. Season with salt and pepper.

Serving Suggestion: Serve the platter with yummy sauce.

Variation Tip: use your favorite fish.

Nutritional Information Per Serving:

Calories 664 | Carbohydrates 11g | Protein 68g | Fat 38g | Sodium 1459mg| Fiber 0.6g

Grilled Halibut

Prep Time: 5 minutes

Cook Time: 10 minutes

Servings: 4

Ingredients

For the halibut

- 4 (4-6-oz.) halibut steaks
- 2 tbsp. extra-virgin olive oil
- Kosher salt
- Freshly ground black pepper

For the mango salsa

- 1 mango, diced
- 1 red pepper, finely chopped
- ½ red onion, diced
- 1 jalapeno, minced
- 1 tbsp. freshly chopped cilantro
- Juice of 1 lime
- Kosher salt
- Freshly ground black pepper

Preparation

1. Preheat Ninja Foodi Grill to medium-high and brush halibut with oil on both sides then season with salt and pepper.

2. Grill halibut until cooked through, about 5 minutes per side.

3. Make salsa: Mix together all ingredients in a medium bowl and season with salt and pepper. Serve salsa over halibut.

Serving Suggestion: Serve the fish with yummy mango salsa.

Variation Tip: Go for regular lime and tomato salsa for fun.

Nutritional Information Per Serving:

Calories 248 | Carbohydrates 40.7g | Protein 2.5g | Fat 10.8g | Sodium 120.4mg| Fiber 0.7g

Ginger Salmon with Cucumber Lime Sauce

Prep Time: 30 minutes

Cook Time: 10 minutes

Servings: 10

Ingredients

- 1 tablespoon grated lime zest
- 4 tsp sugar
- ½ tsp salt
- ¼ cup lime juice
- 2 tbsp olive oil
- 2 tbsp rice vinegar or white wine vinegar
- ½ tsp ground coriander
- ½ tsp freshly ground pepper
- 2 tsp minced fresh ginger root
- 2 garlic cloves, minced
- 2 medium cucumbers, peeled, seeded and chopped
- ⅓ cup chopped fresh cilantro
- 1 tablespoon finely chopped onion

Salmon

- 1 tablespoon olive oil
- ½ tsp salt
- ⅓ cup minced fresh ginger root
- 1 tablespoon lime juice
- ½ tsp freshly ground pepper
- 10 salmon fillets (6 ounces each)

Preparation

1. Place the first 13 Ingredients of the list in a blender. Cover and process until pureed.

2. In a bowl, combine ginger, oil, salt, lime juice, and pepper. Rub over flesh side of salmon fillets.

3. Lightly oil the grill. Place salmon on grill, skin side down. Grill while covered over medium-high heat 10-12 minutes or until fish just begins to flake easily with a fork.

Serving Suggestion: Serve with sauce.

Variation Tip: use chopped dill for garnish.

Nutritional Information per Serving:

Calories 248 | Carbohydrates 40.7g | Protein 2.5g | Fat 10.8g | Sodium 120.4mg| Fiber 0.7g

Grilled Shrimp Cocktail with Yellow Gazpacho Salsa

Prep Time: 40 minutes

Cook Time: 60 minutes

Servings: 4

Ingredients

- 4 medium yellow tomatoes, seeded and finely chopped
- 1 stalk celery, finely chopped
- ½ small red onion, finely chopped
- 1 yellow bell pepper, finely chopped
- 1 medium cucumber, peeled, seeded and finely chopped
- 1 tablespoon Worcestershire sauce
- ½ tsp freshly ground pepper
- 2 tbsp minced fresh chives
- 2 tbsp white-wine vinegar
- 2 tbsp lemon juice
- ¼ tsp salt
- Several dashes hot sauce, to taste
- 1pound raw shrimp, peeled and deveined
- 2 cloves garlic, minced
- 2 tsp minced fresh thyme

Preparation

1. Preheat the grill for eight minutes.

2. Mix the tomatoes, cucumber, celery, bell pepper, onion, vinegar, lemon juice, chives, Worcestershire sauce, salt and pepper, and hot sauce in a big bowl. Cover it and chill for at least twenty minutes or for a single day.

3. Mix the shrimp, garlic, and thyme in a medium bowl; cover it and refrigerate for twenty minutes.

4. Insert grill grates in the unit and close the hood. Select the option GRILL, set the temperature to LOW, and set time to 2 minutes per side. Select the option START/STOP to begin preheating.

Serving Suggestion: Serve the shrimp with salsa in martini glasses.

Variation Tip: use chicken chips with same method.

Nutritional Information Per Serving:

Calories 251.8 | Carbohydrates 33.7g | Protein 2.6g | Fat 12.3g | Sodium 185.7mg| Fiber 0.6g

Garlic Flavored Artichoke Meal

Prep Time: 10 minutes

Cook Time: 10 minutes

Servings: 4

Ingredients

- 2 large artichokes, trimmed and halved
- 3 garlic cloves, chopped
- ½ a lemon, juiced
- ½ cup canola oil
- Salt and pepper to taste

Preparation

1. Select GRILL mode and set your Ninja Foodi Grill to "MAX."
2. Set the timer to 10 minutes.
3. Let it pre-heat until you hear a beep.
4. Add lemon juice, oil, garlic into a medium-sized bowl.
5. Season with salt and pepper.
6. Brush artichoke halves with lemon garlic mix.
7. Once ready, transfer artichokes to Grill.
8. Press them down to maximize grill mark.
9. Grill for 8-10 minutes; make sure to blister on all sides.

Serving Suggestion: Serve with dill garnishing or enjoy as it is.

Variation Tip: use chopped dill for garnish.

Nutritional Information per Serving:

Calories: 285| Fat: 28 g| Fat: 8 g Carbohydrates: 10 g| Fiber: 3 g| Sodium: 137 mg| Protein: 3 g

Honey Carrot Dish

Prep Time: 15 minutes

Cook Time: 10 minutes

Servings: 4

Ingredients

- 6 carrots, cut lengthwise
- 1 tablespoon rosemary, chopped
- 1 tablespoon honey
- 2 tbsp butter, melted

- 1 tablespoon parsley, chopped
- 1 tsp salt

Preparation

1. Take your Ninja Foodi Grill, open the lid.

2. Arrange grill grate and close top.

3. Pre-heat Ninja Foodi by pressing the "GRILL" option and setting it to "MAX.".

4. Then set the timer for 10 minutes.

5. Allow it pre-heat until it sounds a beep.

6. Arrange carrots over the grill grate.

7. Take the remaining Ingredients and spread them.

8. Drizzle honey, lock lid and cook for 5 minutes.

9. Then flip sausages and cook for 5 minutes more.

10. Once done, serve and enjoy!

Serving Suggestion: Serve with dill garnishing or enjoy as it is.

Variation Tip: use chopped dill for garnish.

Nutritional Information per Serving:

Calories: 80|, Fat: 4 g| Carbohydrates: 10 g| Fiber: 3 g| Sodium: 186 mg| Protein: 0.5 g

Mushroom Tomato Roast

Prep Time: 10 minutes

Cook Time: 15 minutes

Servings: 4

Ingredients

- 2 cups cherry tomatoes
- 2 cups cremini button mushrooms
- ¼ cup of vinegar or 1/4 cup of red wine
- 2 garlic cloves, finely chopped
- ½ cup extra-virgin olive oil
- 3 tbsp chopped thyme
- Pinch of crushed red pepper flakes
- 1 tsp kosher salt
- ½ tsp black pepper
- 6 scallions, cut crosswise into 2-inch pieces

Preparation

1. Take a zip-lock bag; add black pepper, salt, red pepper flakes, thyme, vinegar, oil, and garlic. Add mushrooms, tomatoes, and scallions.

2. Shake well and refrigerate for 30-40 minutes to marinate.

3. Take Ninja Foodi Grill, orchestrate it over your kitchen stage, and open the top.

4. Press "Prepare" and alter the temperature to 400°F. Modify the clock to 12 minutes and afterward press "START/STOP." Ninja Foodi will begin preheating.

5. Ninja Foodi is preheated and prepared to cook when it begins to blare. After you hear a blare, open the top.

6. Arrange the mushroom mixture directly inside the pot.

7. Close the top lid and allow it to cook until the timer reads zero.

Serving Suggestion: Serve warm with chilled wine.

Variation Tip: use chopped dill for garnish.

Nutritional Information per Serving:

Calories: 253| Fat: 24g| Carbohydrates: 7g| Fiber: 2g| Sodium: 546mg| Protein: 1g

Tomato Salsa

Prep Time: 5-10 minutes

Cook Time: 10 minutes

Servings: 4

Ingredients

- 1 red onion, peeled, cut in quarters
- 1 jalapeño pepper, cut in half, seeds removed
- 5 Roma tomatoes, cut in half lengthwise
- 1 tablespoon kosher salt
- 2 tsp ground black pepper
- 2 tbsp canola oil
- 1 bunch cilantro, stems trimmed
- Juice and zest of 3 limes
- 3 cloves garlic, peeled
- 2 tbsp ground cumin

Preparation

1. In a blending bowl, join the onion, tomatoes, jalapeño pepper, salt, dark pepper, and canola oil.

2. Take Ninja Foodi Grill, mastermind it over your kitchen stage, and open the top. Mastermind the barbecue mesh and close the top cover.

3. Press "Barbecue" and select the "Maximum" flame broil work. Change the clock to 10 minutes and afterward press "START/STOP." Ninja Foodi will begin preheating.

4. Ninja Foodi is preheated and prepared to cook when it begins to blare. After you hear a signal, open the top cover.

5. Arrange the vegetables over the grill grate.

6. Close the top lid and cook for 5 minutes. Now open the top lid, flip the vegetables.

7. Close the top lid and cook for five more minutes.

8. Blend the mixture in a blender and serve as needed.

Serving Suggestion: Serve with dill garnishing or enjoy as it is.

Variation Tip: use chopped dill for garnish.

Nutritional Information per Serving:

Calories: 169| Fat: 9g|Carbohydrates: 12g| Fiber: 3g| Sodium: 321mg| Protein: 2.5g

Buttery Spinach Meal

Prep Time: 10 minutes

Cook Time: 15 minutes

Servings: 4

Ingredients

- ⅔ cup olives, halved and pitted
- 1 and ½ cups feta cheese, grated
- 4 tbsp butter
- 2pounds spinach, chopped and boiled
- Pepper and salt to taste
- 4 tsp lemon zest, grated

Preparation

1. Take a mixing bowl and add spinach, butter, salt, pepper and mix well.

2. Pre-heat Ninja Foodi by pressing the "AIR CRISP" option and setting it to "340 Degrees F" and timer to 15 minutes.

3. Let it pre-heat until you hear a beep.

4. Arrange a reversible trivet in the Grill Pan, arrange spinach mixture in a basket and place basket in the trivet.

5. Let them roast until the timer runs out.

6. Serve and enjoy!

Serving Suggestion: Serve with your favorite dipping.

Variation Tip: use chopped cilantro for garnish.

Nutritional Information per Serving:

Calories: 250|Fat: 18 g| Carbohydrates: 8 g| Fiber: 3 g| Sodium: 309 mg| Protein: 10 g

Italian Squash Meal

Prep Time: 5-10 minutes

Cook Time: 16 minutes

Servings: 4

Ingredients

- 1 medium butternut squash, peeled, seeded and cut into ½ inch slices
- 1 and ½ tsp oregano, dried
- 1 tsp dried thyme
- 1 tablespoon olive oil

- ½ tsp salt
- ¼ tsp black pepper

Preparation

1. Add slices alongside other Ingredients into a mixing bowl.

2. Mix them well.

3. Pre-heat your Ninja Foodi by pressing the "GRILL" option and setting it to "MED.".

4. Set the timer to 16 minutes.

5. Allow it to pre-heat until it beep.

6. Arrange squash slices over the grill grate.

7. Cook for 8 minutes.

8. Flip and cook for 8 minutes more.

9. Serve and enjoy!

Serving Suggestion: Serve warm and enjoy.

Variation Tip: use chopped dill for garnish.

Nutritional Information per Serving:

Calories: 238| Fat: 12 g| Carbohydrates: 36 g| Fiber: 3 g| Sodium: 128 mg| Protein: 15 g

Cool Rosemary Potatoes

Prep Time: 10 minutes

Cook Time: 20 minutes

Servings: 4

Ingredients

- 2pounds baby red potatoes, quartered
- ½ tsp parsley, dried
- ¼ tsp celery powder
- 2 tbsp extra virgin olive oil
- ¼ cup onion flakes, dried
- ½ tsp garlic powder
- ½ tsp onion powder
- ½ tsp salt
- ¼ tsp freshly ground black pepper

Preparation

1. Add all listed Ingredients into a large bowl.

2. Toss well and coat them well.

3. Pre-heat your Ninja Foodi by pressing the "AIR CRISP" option and setting it to 390 Degrees F.

4. Set the timer to 20 minutes.

5. Allow it to pre-heat until it beeps.

6. Once preheated, add potatoes to the cooking basket.

7. Close the lid and cook for 10 minutes.

8. Shake the basket and cook for 10 minutes more.

9. Check the crispness if it is done or not.

10. Cook for 5 minutes more if needed.

11. Serve and enjoy!

Serving Suggestion: Serve with chilled beer.

Variation Tip: use shredded cheese for extra flavor.

Nutritional Information per Serving:

Calories: 232| Fat: 7 g| Carbohydrates: 39 g| Fiber: 6 g| Sodium: 249 mg| Protein: 4 g

Cheddar Cauliflower Meal

Prep Time: 5-10 minutes

Cook Time: 15 minutes

Servings: 2

Ingredients

- ½ tsp garlic powder
- ½ tsp paprika
- Ocean salt and ground dark pepper to taste
- 1 head cauliflower, stemmed and leaves removed
- 1 cup Cheddar cheese, shredded
- Ranch dressing, for garnish
- ¼ cup canola oil or vegetable oil
- 2 tbsp chopped chives
- 4 slices bacon, cooked and crumbled

Preparation

1. Cut the cauliflower into 2-inch pieces.

2. In a blending bowl, include the oil, garlic powder, and paprika. Season with salt and ground dark pepper; join well. Coat the florets with the blend.

3. Take Ninja Foodi Grill, mastermind it over your kitchen stage, and open the top cover.

4. Mastermind the flame broil mesh and close the top cover.

5. Press "Flame broil" and select the "Maximum" barbecue work. Change the clock to 15 minutes and afterward press "START/STOP." Ninja Foodi will begin preheating.

6. Ninja Foodi is preheated and prepared to cook when it begins to signal. After you hear a blare, open the top.

7. Organize the pieces over the flame broil grind.

8. Close the top lid and cook for 10 minutes. Now open the top lid, flip the pieces and top with the cheese.

9. Close the top lid and cook for 5 more minutes.

Serving Suggestion: Serve warm with the chives and ranch dressing on top.

Variation Tip: use chili flakes for spice.

Nutritional Information per Serving:

Calories: 534| Fat: 34g |Carbohydrates: 14.5g| Fiber: 4g| Sodium: 1359mg| Protein: 31g

Delicious Broccoli and Arugula

Prep Time: 10 minutes

Cook Time: 12 minutes

Servings: 4

Ingredients

- Pepper as needed
- ½ tsp salt
- Red pepper flakes
- 2 tbsp extra virgin olive oil
- 1 tablespoon canola oil
- ½ red onion, sliced
- 1 garlic clove, minced
- 1 tsp Dijon mustard
- 1 tsp honey
- 1 tablespoon lemon juice
- 2 tbsp parmesan cheese, grated
- 4 cups arugula, torn
- 2 heads broccoli, trimmed

Preparation

1. Pre-heat your Ninja Foodi Grill to MAX and set the timer to 12 minutes.

2. Take a large-sized bowl and add broccoli, sliced onion, and canola oil, toss the mixture well until coated.

3. Once you hear the beep, it is pre-heated.

4. Arrange your vegetables over the grill grate; let them grill for 8-12 minutes.

5. Take a medium-sized bowl and whisk in lemon juice, olive oil, mustard, honey, garlic, red pepper flakes, pepper, and salt.

6. Once done, add the prepared veggies and arugula in a bowl.

7. Drizzle the prepared vinaigrette on top, sprinkle a bit of parmesan.

8. Stir and mix.

9. Enjoy!

Serving Suggestion: Serve warm with favorite drink.

Variation Tip: use cheese for taste.

Nutritional Information per Serving:

Calories: 168| Fat: 12 g| Carbohydrates: 13 g| Fiber: 1 g| Sodium: 392 mg| Protein: 6 g

Honey Dressed Asparagus

Prep Time: 5-10 minutes

Cook Time: 15 minutes

Servings: 4

Ingredients

- 2pounds asparagus, trimmed
- 4 tbsp tarragon, minced
- ¼ cup honey
- 2 tbsp olive oil
- 1 tsp salt
- ½ tsp pepper

Preparation

1. Add asparagus, oil, salt, honey, pepper, tarragon into your bowl, Toss them well.

2. Pre-heat your Ninja Foodi by pressing the "GRILL" option and setting it to "MED.".

3. Set the timer to 8 minutes.

4. Allow it pre-heat until it makes a beep sound.

5. Arrange asparagus over grill grate and lock lid.

6. Cook for 4 minutes.

7. Then flip asparagus and cook for 4 minutes more.

8. Serve and enjoy!

Serving Suggestion: Serve warm and enjoy.

Variation Tip: use chili flakes for extra spice.

Nutritional Information per Serving:

Calories: 240| Fat: 15 g| Carbohydrates: 31 g| Fiber: 1 g| Sodium: 103 mg| Protein: 7 g

Mustard Green Veggie Meal

Prep Time: 10 minutes

Cook Time: 30-40 minutes

Servings: 4

Ingredients

Vinaigrette

- 2 tbsp Dijon mustard
- 1 tsp salt
- ¼ tsp black pepper
- ½ cup avocado oil
- ½ olive oil
- ½ cup red wine vinegar

- 2 tbsp honey

Veggies

- 4 sweet onions, quartered
- 4 yellow squash, cut in half
- 4 red peppers, seeded and halved
- 4 zucchinis, halved
- 2 bunches green onions, trimmed

Preparation

1. Take a small bowl and whisk mustard, pepper, honey, vinegar, and salt.

2. Add oil to make a smooth mixture.

3. Mastermind the flame broil mesh and close the top cover.

4. Pre-heat Ninja Foodi by pressing the "GRILL" option and setting it to "MED" and timer to 10 minutes.

5. Let it pre-heat until you hear a beep.

6. Arrange the onion quarters over the grill grate, lock lid and cook for 5 minutes.

7. Flip the peppers and cook for 5 minutes more.

8. Grill the other vegetables in the same manner with 7 minutes each side for zucchini, pepper, and squash and 1 minute for onion.

9. Prepare the vinaigrette by mixing all the Ingredients under vinaigrette in a bowl.

Serving Suggestion: Serve the grilled veggies with vinaigrette on top.

Variation Tip: use your favorite veggies for fun.

Nutritional Information per Serving:

Calories: 326| Fat: 4.5 g| Carbohydrates: 35 g| Fiber: 4 g| Sodium: 543 mg| Protein: 8 g

Hearty Spinach Olive

Prep Time: 5-10 minutes

Cook Time: 15 minutes

Servings: 3

Ingredients

- 2 pounds spinach, chopped and boiled
- 1 and ½ cups feta cheese, grated
- 4 tbsp butter
- ⅔ cup olives, halved and pitted
- 4 tsp lemon zest, grated
- Pepper and salt to taste

Preparation

1. Add spinach, butter, salt, pepper into a mixing bowl, Mix them well.

2. Pre-heat your Ninja Foodi by pressing the "AIR CRISP" option and setting it to 340 Degrees F.

3. Set the timer to 15 minutes.

4. Allow it to pre-heat until it beeps.

5. Arrange a reversible trivet in the Grill Pan.

6. Arrange spinach mixture in a basket and place basket in the trivet.

7. Let them roast for 15 minutes.

8. Serve and enjoy!

Serving Suggestion: Serve with chilled drink.

Variation Tip: add honey for extra fun.

Nutritional Information per Serving:

Calories: 250| Fat: 18 g| Carbohydrates: 8 g| Fiber: 4 g| Sodium: 339 mg| Protein: 10 g

Air Grilled Brussels

Prep Time: 5-10 minutes

Cook Time: 12 minutes

Servings: 4

Ingredients

- 6 slices bacon, chopped
- 1 pound Brussel sprouts, halved
- 2 tbsp olive oil, extra virgin
- 1 tsp salt
- ½ tsp black pepper, ground

Preparation

1. Add Brussels, olive oil, salt, pepper, and bacon into a mixing bowl.

2. Pre-heat Ninja Foodi by pressing the "AIR CRISP" option and setting it to "390 degrees F.".

3. Set the timer to 12 minutes.

4. Allow it to pre-heat until it beeps.

5. Arrange Brussels over basket and lock lid.

6. Cook for 6 minutes.

7. Shake it and cook for 6 minutes more.

8. Serve and enjoy!

Serving Suggestion: Serve with chilled drink.

Variation Tip: use chopped dill for garnish.

Nutritional Information per Serving:

Calories: 279| Fat: 18 g| Carbohydrates: 12 g| Fiber: 4 g| Sodium: 874 mg| Protein: 1 g

Delicious Grilled Honey Fruit Salad

Prep Time: 5-10 minutes

Cook Time: 5 minutes

Servings: 4

Ingredients

- 1 tablespoon lime juice, freshly squeezed
- 6 tbsp honey, divided
- 2 peaches, pitted and sliced
- 1 can (9 ounces) pineapple chunks, drained and juiced reserved
- ½ pound strawberries washed, hulled, and halved

Preparation

1. Take a shallow mixing bowl, then add respectively soy sauce, balsamic vinegar, oil, maple syrup and whisk well.

2. Then add broccoli and keep it aside.

3. Press the "GRILL" of the Ninja Foodi Grill and set it to "MAX" mode with 10 minutes timer.

4. Keep it in the preheating process.

5. When you hear a beat, add broccoli over the grill grate.

6. After then lock the lid and cook until the timer shows 0.

7. Lastly, garnish the food with pepper flakes and sesame seeds.

8. Enjoy!

Serving Suggestion: Serve topped with sesame seeds and pepper flakes.

Variation Tip: use chopped dill for garnish.

Nutritional Information per Serving:

Calories: 141| Fat: 7 g| Carbohydrate: 14 g| Fiber: 4 g| Sodium: 853 mg| Protein: 4 g

Lovely Seasonal Broccoli

Prep Time: 10 minutes

Cook Time: 10 minutes

Servings: 4

Ingredients

- ½ tsp salt
- ½ tsp red chili powder
- ¼ tsp spice mix
- 2 tbsp yogurt
- 1 tablespoon chickpea flour

- ¼ tsp turmeric powder
- 1pound broccoli, cut into florets

Preparation

1. Take your florets and wash them thoroughly.

2. Take a bowl and add listed Ingredients, except the florets.

3. Add broccoli and combine the mix well; let the mixture sit for 30 minutes.

4. Pre-heat your Ninja Foodi to AIR CRISP mode at 390 degrees F and set the timer to 10 minutes.

5. Once you hear a beep, add florets and crisp for 10 minutes.

Serving Suggestion: Serve warm.

Variation Tip: use shredded cheese for taste.

Nutritional Information per Serving:

Calories: 111|Fat: 2 g| Carbohydrates: 12 g| Fiber: 1 g| Sodium: 024 mg| Protein: 7 g

Mammamia Banana Boats

Prep Time: 19 minutes

Cook Time: 6 minutes

Servings: 4

Ingredients

- ½ cup peanut butter chips
- ½ cup of chocolate chips
- 1 cup mini marshmallows
- 4 ripe bananas

Preparation

1. With the peel, slice a banana lengthwise and remember that not to cut all the way through.

2. Onward, reveal the inside of the banana by using your hand.

3. Press the "GRILL" option and set this in "MEDIUM" to pre-heat Ninja Foodi with a 6 minutes timer.

4. Until you hear a beep, keep it in the pre-heat process.

5. Put the banana over the Grill Grate and lock the lid, let it cook for 4-6 minutes until chocolate melts and bananas are toasted.

6. Serve and Enjoy!

Serving Suggestion: Serve with melted chocolate.

Variation Tip: Uses condense milk as topping.

Nutritional Information per Serving:

Calories: 505| Fat: 18 g| Carbohydrates: 82 g| Fiber: 6 g | Sodium: 166 mg| Protein: 10 g

Grilled Sweet Honey Carrot

Prep Time: 10 minutes

Cook Time: 10 minutes

Servings: 6

Ingredients

- 1 tsp salt
- 1 tablespoon honey
- 1 tablespoon rosemary, chopped
- 1 tablespoon parsley, chopped
- 6 carrots, cut lengthwise
- 2 tbsp butter, melted

Preparation

1. Pre-heat your Ninja Foodi Grill to MAX, set a timer for 10 minutes.

2. Once you hear the beep, arrange carrots over the grill grate.

3. Spread remaining Ingredients and drizzle honey.

4. Lock lid and cook for 5 minutes, flip and cook for 5 minutes more.

Serving Suggestion: Serve and enjoy.

Variation Tip: use chopped dill for garnish.

Nutritional Information per Serving:

Calories: 80| Fat: 4 g| Carbohydrates: 10 g| Fiber: 3 g| Sodium: 186 mg| Protein: 0.5 g

Complete Italian Squash

Prep Time: 5-10 minutes

Cook Time: 16 minutes

Servings: 4

Ingredients

- ¼ tsp black pepper
- 1 and ½ tsp dried oregano
- 1 tablespoon olive oil
- ½ tsp salt
- 1 tsp dried thyme
- 1 medium butternut squash, peeled, seeded, and cut into ½ inch slices

Preparation

1. Take a mixing bowl and add slices and other Ingredients, mix well.

2. Pre-heat your Ninja Foodi Grill to MED and set the timer to 16 minutes.

3. Once you hear the beep, arrange squash slices over the grill grate.

4. Cook for 8 minutes, flip and cook for 8 minutes.

Serving Suggestion: Serve warm.

Variation Tip: use shredded cheese for extra taste.

Nutritional Information per Serving:

Calories: 238| Fat: 12 g| Carbohydrates: 36 g| Fiber: 3 g| Sodium: 128 mg| Protein: 15 g

Eggplant and Tomato Meal

Prep Time: 10 minutes

Cook Time: 14 minutes

Servings: 4

Ingredients

- 1 eggplant, sliced and ¼ inch thick
- ½ pound buffalo mozzarella, sliced into ¼ inch thick
- 2 heirloom tomatoes, cut into ¼ inch thick
- 12 large basil leaves
- 2 tablespoons canola oil
- Salt to taste

Preparation

1. Add eggplant, oil into a large-sized bowl.

2. Toss them well.

3. Pre-heat Ninja Foodi by pressing the "GRILL" option and setting it to "MAX.".

4. Set the timer to 15 minutes.

5. Let it pre-heat until you hear a beep.

6. Transfer eggplants to Grill Plant and lock lid.

7. Cook for 8-12 minutes.

8. Once done, top eggplant with one slice of tomato and mozzarella.

9. Lock lid and cook for 2 minutes more until cheese melts.

10. Once done, remove eggplant from the Grill.

11. Place 2-3 basil leaves on top of half stack.

12. Place remaining eggplant stacks on top with basil.

13. Season with salt and garnish with remaining basil.

14. Serve and enjoy!

Serving Suggestion: serve with basil.

Variation Tip: use chives for taste.

Nutritional Information per Serving:

Calories: 100| Fat: 19 g| Carbohydrates: 11 g| Fiber: 4 g| Sodium: 1555 mg| Protein: 32 g

Crispy Brussels

Prep Time: 5-10 minutes

Cook Time: 12 minutes

Servings: 4

Ingredients

- 1 pound Brussels sprouts, halved
- 6 slices bacon, chopped
- 2 tbsp olive oil, extra virgin
- 1 tsp salt
- ½ tsp ground black pepper

Preparation

1. Add Brussels, bacon, olive oil, salt, and pepper into a mixing bowl.

2. Pre-heat Ninja Foodi by pressing the "AIR CRISP" option and setting it to "390 degrees F.".

3. Set the timer to 12 minutes.

4. Let it pre-heat until you hear a beep.

5. Arrange Brussels over basket and lock lid.

6. Cook for 6 minutes.

7. Shake it generously and cook for 6 minutes more.

Serving Suggestion: Serve warm and crispy.

Variation Tip: use chopped dill for flavor.

Nutritional Information per Serving:

Calories: 279| Fat: 18 g| Carbohydrates: 12 g| Fiber: 4 g| Sodium: 874 mg| Protein: 14 g

Broccoli Maple Grill

Prep Time: 5-10 minutes

Cook Time: 10 minutes

Servings: 4

Ingredients

- 2 tsp maple syrup
- 4 tablespoons balsamic vinegar
- 2 tablespoon canola oil
- 4 tbsp soy sauce
- 2 heads broccoli, cut into floret
- Pepper flakes and sesame seeds for garnish

Preparation

1. Take a shallow mixing bowl, then add respectively soy sauce, balsamic vinegar, oil, maple syrup and whisk well.

2. Then add broccoli and keep it aside.

3. Press the "GRILL" of the Ninja Foodi Grill and set it to "MAX" mode with 10 minutes timer.

4. Keep it in the preheating process.

5. When you hear a beat, add broccoli over the grill grate.

6. After then lock the lid and cook until the timer shows 0.

7. Lastly, garnish the food with pepper flakes and sesame seeds.

Serving Suggestion: Serve topped with sesame seeds and chili flakes.

Variation Tip: use chopped dill for garnish.

Nutritional Information per Serving:

Calories: 141| Fat: 7 g| Carbohydrate: 14 g| Fiber: 4 g| Sodium: 853 mg| Protein: 4 g

Creamed Potato Corns

Prep Time: 5-10 minutes

Cook Time: 30-40 minutes

Servings: 4

Ingredients

- 1 and ½ tsp garlic salt
- ½ cup sour cream
- 1 jalapeno pepper, seeded and minced
- 1 tablespoon lime juice
- 1 tsp ground cumin
- ½ cup milk
- 2 pobiano pepper
- ¼ tsp cayenne pepper
- 2 sweet corn years
- 1 tablespoon cilantro, minced
- 3 tbsp olive oil

Preparation

1. Drain potatoes and rub them with oil.

2. Pre-heat your Ninja Foodi Grill to MED, setting a timer for 10 minutes.

3. Once you hear the beep, arrange poblano peppers over the grill grate.

4. Let them cook for 5 minutes, flip and cook for 5 minutes more.

5. Grill remaining veggies in the same way, giving 7 minutes to each side.

6. Take a bowl and whisk in the remaining Ingredients and prepare your vinaigrette.

7. Peel grilled corn and chop them.

8. Divide ears into small pieces and cut the potatoes.

Serving Suggestion: Serve grilled veggies with vinaigrette.

Variation Tip: use chopped dill for garnish.

Nutritional Information per Serving:

Calories: 344| Fat: 5 g| Carbohydrates: 51 g| Fiber: 3 g| Sodium: 600 mg| Protein: 5 g

Spice Lover's Cajun Eggplant

Prep Time: 5-10 minutes

Cook Time: 12 minutes

Servings: 4

Ingredients

- 2 small eggplants, cut into slices
- 3 tsp Cajun seasoning
- ¼ cup olive oil
- 2 tbsp lime juice

Preparation

1. Coat eggplant slices with oil, lemon juice, and Cajun seasoning in a mixing bowl.
2. Take your Ninja Foodi Grill and press "GRILL," and set to "MED" mode.
3. Set the timer to 10 minutes.
4. Let it pre-heat until you hear a beep.
5. Arrange eggplants over grill grate and lock lid.
6. Cook for 5 minutes.
7. Flip and cook for 5 minutes more.

Serving Suggestion: Serve with dill garnishing or enjoy as it is.

Variation Tip: use chopped dill for garnish.

Nutritional Information per Serving:

Calories: 362| Fat: 11 g| Carbohydrates: 16 g| Fiber: 1 g |Sodium: 694 mg| Protein: 8 g

Grilled Honey Carrots

Prep Time: 15 minutes

Cook Time: 10 minutes

Servings: 4

Ingredients

- 6 carrots, cut lengthwise
- 1 tablespoon rosemary, chopped
- 2 tbsp melted butter
- 1 tablespoon parsley, chopped
- 1 tablespoon honey
- 1 tsp salt

Preparation

1. Take your Ninja Foodi Grill and open the lid.

2. Arrange grill grate and close top.

3. Pre-heat Ninja Foodi by pressing the "GRILL" option and setting it to "MAX."

4. Set the timer to 10 minutes.

5. Let it pre-heat until you hear a beep.

6. Arrange carrots over grill grate and spread the remaining Ingredients, and drizzle honey.

7. Lock lid and cook for 5 minutes.

8. Flip sausages and cook for 5 minutes more.

Serving Suggestion: Serve with dill garnishing or enjoy as it is.

Variation Tip: use chopped dill for garnish.

Nutritional Information per Serving:

Calories: 80| Fat: 4 g| Carbohydrates: 10 g| Fiber: 3 g| Sodium: 186 mg| Protein: 0.5 g

Honey-Luscious Asparagus

Prep Time: 5-10 minutes

Cook Time: 15 minutes

Servings: 4

Ingredients

- 2pounds asparagus, trimmed
- 4 tbsp tarragon, minced
- ¼ cup honey
- 2 tbsp olive oil
- 1 tsp salt
- ½ tsp pepper

Preparation

1. Add asparagus, oil, salt, honey, pepper, tarragon into a mixing bowl.

2. Toss them well.

3. Pre-heat Ninja Foodi by pressing the "GRILL" option and setting it to "MED."

4. Set the timer to 8 minutes.

5. Let it pre-heat until you hear a beep.

6. Arrange asparagus over grill grate and lock lid.

7. Cook for 4 minutes.

8. Flip the asparagus and cook for 4 minutes more.

Serving Suggestion: Serve with dill garnishing or enjoy as it is.

Variation Tip: use shredded cheese for fun.

Nutritional Information per Serving:

Calories: 240| Fat: 15 g| Carbohydrates: 31 g| Fiber: 1 g| Sodium: 103 mg| Protein: 7 g

Honey Touched Bratwurst

Prep Time: 5-10 minutes

Cook Time: 10 minutes

Servings: 4

Ingredients

- ¼ cup honey
- 1 tsp steak sauce
- 2 tbsp mayonnaise
- 4 brat buns, split
- ¼ cup Dijon mustard
- 4 bratwurst links, uncooked

Preparation

1. First, mix the mustard with steak sauce and mayonnaise in a bowl.

2. Prepare and pre-heat the Ninja Foodi Grill on a High-temperature setting.

3. Once it is pre-heated, open the lid and place the bratwurst on the Grill.

4. Cover the Ninja Foodi Grill's lid and Grill on the "Grilling Mode" for 10 minutes per side until their internal temperature reaches 320 degrees F.

Serving Suggestion: Serve with buns and mustard sauce on top.

Variation Tip: use cheese for flavor.

Nutritional Information per Serving:

Calories: 225| Fat: 17 g| Carbohydrates: 13 g| Fiber: 3 g| Sodium: 284 mg| Protein: 6 g

Lovely Rum Sundae

Prep Time: 10 minutes

Cook Time: 8 minutes

Servings: 4

Ingredients

- Vanilla ice cream for serving
- 1 pineapple, cored and sliced
- 1 tsp cinnamon, ground
- ½ cup brown sugar, packed
- ½ cup dark rum

Preparation:

1. Take a large deep bowl and add sugar, cinnamon, and rum.

2. Add the pineapple in the layer, dredge them properly and make sure that they are coated well.

3. Pre-heat your Foodi in "GRILL" mode with "MAX" settings, setting the timer to 8 minutes.

4. Once you hear the beep, strain any additional rum from the pineapple slices and transfer them to the grill rate of your appliance.

5. Press them down and grill for 6- 8 minutes. Make sure not to overcrowd the grill grate, Cook in batches if needed.

Serving Suggestion: Serve Top each of the ring with a scoop of your favorite ice cream, sprinkle a bit of cinnamon on top.

Variation Tip: use melted chocolate for extra taste.

Nutritional Information per Serving:

Calories: 240| Fat: 4 g| Carbohydrates: 43 g| Fiber: 8 g| Sodium: 85 mg| Protein: 2 g

The Healthy Granola Bites

Prep Time: 10 minutes

Cook Time: 15-20 minutes

Servings: 4

Ingredients

- Salt and pepper to taste
- 1 tablespoon coriander
- A handful of thyme, diced
- ¼ cup of coconut milk
- 3 handful of cooked vegetables, your choice

- 3 pounces plain granola

Preparation

1. Pre-heat your Ninja Foodi to 352 degrees F in AIR CRISP mode, set a timer to 20 minutes.

2. Take a bowl and add your cooked vegetables, granola.

3. Use an immersion blender to blitz your granola until you have a nice breadcrumb-like consistency.

4. Add coconut milk to the mix and mix until you have a nice firm texture.

5. Use the mixture to make granola balls and transfer them to your Grill.

6. Cook for 20 minutes.

7. Serve and enjoy!

Serving Suggestion: Serve and enjoy.

Variation Tip: add dates for sweetness.

Nutritional Information per Serving:

Calories: 140| Fat: 10 g| Carbohydrates: 14 g| Fiber: 4 g| Sodium: 215 mg| Protein: 2 g

Marshmallow Banana Boat

Prep Time: 19 minutes

Cook Time: 6 minutes

Servings: 4

Ingredients

- 4 ripe bananas
- 1 cup mini marshmallows
- ½ cup of chocolate chips
- ½ cup peanut butter chips

Preparation

1. Slice a banana lengthwise, keeping its peel.

2. Use your hands to open banana peel like a book, revealing the inside of a banana.

3. Divide marshmallow, chocolate chips, peanut butter among bananas, stuffing them inside/

4. Preheat Ninja Foodie by pressing the "GRILL" option and setting it to "MEDIUM" and timer to 6 minutes let it preheat until you hear a beep.

5. Transfer banana to Grill Grate and lock lid, cook for 4-6 minutes until chocolate melts and bananas are toasted.

Serving Suggestion: Serve and enjoy.

Variation Tip: use nuts for crunch.

Nutritional Information per Serving:

Calories: 505| Fat: 18 g| Carbohydrates: 82| Fiber: 6 g| Sodium: 103 mg| Protein: 10 g

Rummy Pineapple Sunday

Prep Time: 10 minutes

Cook Time: 8 minutes

Servings: 4

Ingredients

- ½ cup dark rum
- ½ cup packed brown sugar
- 1 pineapple cored and sliced
- Vanilla ice cream, for serving

Preparation

1. Take a large-sized bowl and add rum, sugar, cinnamon.

2. Add pineapple slices, arrange them in the layer. Coat mixture then let them soak for 5 minutes, per side.

3. Preheat Ninja Foodie by pressing the "GRILL" option and setting it to "MAX" and timer to 8 minutes.

4. Let it preheat until you hear a beep.

5. Strain extra rum sauce from pineapple.

6. Transfer prepared fruit in grill grate in a single layer, press down fruit and lock lid.

7. Grill for 6-8 minutes without flipping, work in batches if needed.

8. Once done, remove and serve.

Serving Suggestion: top each pineapple ring with a scoop of ice cream, sprinkle cinnamon and serve Enjoy!

Variation Tip: use melted chocolate for taste.

Nutritional Information per Serving:

Calories: 240| Fat: 4 g| Carbohydrates: 43 g| Fiber: 3 g| Sodium: 32 mg| Protein: 2 g

Lovely Rum Sundae

Prep Time: 10 minutes

Cook Time: 8 minutes

Servings: 4

Ingredients

- Vanilla ice cream for serving
- 1 pineapple, cored and sliced
- 1 tsp cinnamon, ground
- ½ cup brown sugar, packed

- ½ cup dark rum

Preparation

1. Take a large deep bowl and add sugar, cinnamon, and rum.

2. Add the pineapple in the layer, dredge them properly and make sure that they are coated well.

3. Pre-heat your Foodi in "GRILL" mode with "MAX" settings, setting the timer to 8 minutes.

4. Once you hear the beep, strain any additional rum from the pineapple slices and transfer them to the grill rate of your appliance.

5. Press them down and grill for 6- 8 minutes. Make sure to not overcrowd the grill grate, cook in batches if needed.

Serving Suggestion: Serve Top each of the ring with a scoop of your favorite ice cream, sprinkle a bit of cinnamon on top.

Variation Tip: use liquid chocolate for taste.

Nutritional Information per Serving:

Calories: 240| Fat: 4 g| Carbohydrates: 43 g| Fiber: 8 g| Sodium: 85 mg| Protein: 2 g

Cute Marshmallow and Banana

Prep Time: 19 minutes

Cook Time: 6 minutes

Servings: 4

Ingredients

- 4 ripe bananas
- 1 cup mini marshmallows
- ½ cup of chocolate chips
- ½ cup peanut butter chips

Preparation

1. Slice a banana lengthwise, keeping its peel. Ensure not to cut all the way through.

2. Use your hands to open banana peel like a book, revealing the inside of a banana.

3. Divide marshmallow, chocolate chips, peanut butter among bananas, stuffing them inside.

4. Pre-heat Ninja Foodi by pressing the "GRILL" option and setting it to "MEDIUM" and timer to 6 minutes.

5. Let it pre-heat until you hear a beep.

6. Transfer banana to Grill Grate and lock lid, cook for 4-6 minutes until chocolate melts and bananas are toasted.

Serving Suggestion: Serve and enjoy.

Variation Tip: use chocolate shavings for little crunch.

Nutritional Information per Serving:

Calories: 505| Fat: 18 g| Carbohydrates: 82 g| Fiber: 6 g| Sodium: 103 mg| Protein: 10 g

Grilled Apples with Bourbon and Brown Sugar

Prep Time: 20 minutes.
Cook Time: 7 minutes.
Serves: 4

Ingredients

- 1 packet Brown Sugar Bourbon Marinade
- ½ cup oil
- ½cup water
- 2 tbsp apple cider vinegar
- 4 apples
- ½ tsp cinnamon
- 1 cup vanilla ice cream
- ¼cup granola

Preparation

1. Prepare the Brown Sugar Bourbon Marinade by whisking together the water, oil, and apple cider vinegar. Pour the marinade into a large pan or zip top bag.

2. Remove the cores from the four apples with an apple corer.

3. Cut the apples horizontally into thick ½-inch slices. Discard the top and bottom. You should get 2-3 apple slices per apple depending on the size of your apples.

4. Place the apple slices in the marinade and turn or toss to gently coat. Cover and allow marinating for 15 minutes, but no longer than 30 minutes.

5. Preheat your grill to 350°F or medium high.

6. Using tongs, place the apple slices onto the hot grill. Allow to grill for 2-3 minutes or until light brown grill marks appear on the bottoms.

7. Turn and grill an additional 2-3 minutes or until the apples are just fork-tender.

8. Remove to a plate and allow cooling a few minutes.

Serving Suggestion: Top the 2-3 slices of the warm apples with a sprinkle of cinnamon, a scoop of vanilla ice cream, and granola. Serve immediately.

Variation Tip: add pears and have unique deliciousness.

Nutritional Information Per Serving:

Calories 199 | Fat 5g | Carbohydrates 38g| Fiber 5g | Sodium 31mg | Protein 3g

Chocolate Cheesecake

Prep Time: 15 minutes

Cook Time: 15 minutes

Servings: 4

Ingredients

- 2 cups cream cheese, softened
- 2 eggs
- 2 tsp cocoa powder
- 1 tsp pure vanilla extract
- ½ cup Swerve

Preparation

1. Add in eggs, cocoa powder, vanilla extract, swerve, cream cheese in an immersion blender and blend until smooth.

2. Pour the mixture evenly into mason jars.

3. Put the mason jars in the insert of Ninja Foodi and close the lid.

4. Select "Bake/Roast" and bake for 15 minutes at 360 degrees F.

5. Refrigerate for at least 2 hours.

Serving Suggestion: Serve and enjoy.

Variation Tip: use chopped nuts for garnish.

Nutritional Information per Serving:

Calories 244| Total Fat 24 g| Carbohydrates2.1 g| Fiber 0.1 g| Sodium 204 mg| Protein 4 g

Lemon Mousse

Prep Time: 15 minutes

Cook Time: 12 minutes

Servings: 2

Ingredients

- 4-ounce cream cheese softened
- ½ cup heavy cream
- ⅛ cup fresh lemon juice
- ½ tsp lemon liquid stevia
- 2 pinches salt

Preparation

15. Take a bowl and mix cream cheese, heavy cream, lemon juice, salt, and stevia.

16. Pour this mixture into the ramekins and transfer the ramekins in the pot of Ninja Foodi.

17. Select "Bake/Roast" and bake for 12 minutes at 350 degrees F.

Serving Suggestion: Pour into the serving glasses and refrigerate for at least 3 hours and serve.

Variation Tip: use orange juice for flavor.

Nutritional Information per Serving:

Calories: 225| Fat: 17 g| Carbohydrates: 13 g| Fiber: 3 g| Sodium: 284 mg| Protein: 6 g

4 WEEKS MEAL PLAN

Week 1

DAY1	**BREAKFAST**	Homely Zucchini Muffin
	LUNCH	Peach BBQ Chicken Thighs
	SNACKS	Great Mac and Cheese Bowl
	DINNER	Grilled BBQ Turkey
DAY2	**BREAKFAST**	Ninja Food Bean
	LUNCH	Moroccan Roast Chicken
	SNACKS	Delicious Grilled Honey Fruit Salad
	DINNER	Spinach Salad with Steak & Blueberries
DAY3	**BREAKFAST**	Kale and Sausage Delight
	LUNCH	Grilled Shrimp Cocktail with Yellow Gazpacho Salsa
	SNACKS	Lovely Seasonal Broccoli
	DINNER	Sweet and Sour Chicken BBQ
DAY4	**BREAKFAST**	Energetic Bagel Platter
	LUNCH	Greek Chicken with Tzatziki Sauce
	SNACKS	Mammamia Banana Boats
	DINNER	Bourbon Pork Chops
DAY5	**BREAKFAST**	Butternut Squash with Italian Herbs
	LUNCH	Juicy Stuffed Bell Peppers
	SNACKS	Grilled Sweet Honey Carrot

	DINNER	Alfredo Chicken Apples
DAY6	**BREAKFAST**	Mushroom Pepper
	LUNCH	Chipotle-Raspberry Pork Chops
	SNACKS	Complete Italian Squash
	DINNER	Grilled Beef Burgers
DAY7	**BREAKFAST**	Stuffed Up Bacon and Pepper
	LUNCH	Delicious Pot Roast
	SNACKS	Eggplant and Tomato Meal
	DINNER	The Tarragon Chicken Meal

Week 2

	BREAKFAST	Epic Breakfast Burrito
DAY1	**LUNCH**	Steak Pineapple Mania
	SNACKS	Crispy Brussels
	DINNER	Hearty Chicken Zucchini Kabobs
DAY2	**BREAKFAST**	Simple Zucchini Egg Muffins
	LUNCH	Steak Kabobs
	SNACKS	Broccoli Maple Grill
	DINNER	Turmeric Pork Chops with Green Onion Rice
DAY3	**BREAKFAST**	The Broccoli and Maple Mix
	LUNCH	Minted Tomato, Onion & Glazed Tofu Kebabs
	SNACKS	Creamed Potato Corns

	DINNER	Daisy Fresh Maple Chicken
DAY4	**BREAKFAST**	Veggie Packed Egg Muffin
	LUNCH	Chicken Satay
	SNACKS	Spice Lover's Cajun Eggplant
	DINNER	Lettuce Cheese Steak
DAY5	**BREAKFAST**	Morning Frittata
	LUNCH	Steak and Potatoes
	SNACKS	Grilled Honey Carrot
	DINNER	Chicken Chili and Beans
DAY6	**BREAKFAST**	Ninja Food Bean
	LUNCH	BBQ Beef Short Ribs
	SNACKS	Honey-Luscious Asparagus
	DINNER	Grilled Pork Tenderloin Marinated in Spicy Soy Sauce
DAY7	**BREAKFAST**	Kale and Sausage Delight
	LUNCH	Chicken & Bacon Caesar Salad
	SNACKS	Honey Touched Bratwurst
	DINNER	Ginger Salmon with Cucumber Lime Sauce

Week 3

	BREAKFAST	Veggie Packed Egg Muffin
DAY1	**LUNCH**	Broccoli and Arugula Salad
	SNACKS	Honey Touched Bratwurst

	DINNER	Avocado Salsa Steak
DAY2	**BREAKFAST**	The Broccoli and Maple Mix
	LUNCH	Honey Dressed Asparagus
	SNACKS	Honey-Luscious Asparagus
	DINNER	Sausage and Pepper Grinders
DAY3	**BREAKFAST**	Epic Breakfast Burrito
	LUNCH	Mustard Green Veggie Meal
	SNACKS	Grilled Honey Carrots
	DINNER	Grilled Steak Salad with Tomatoes & Eggplant
DAY4	**BREAKFAST**	Energetic Bagel Platter
	LUNCH	Hearty Spinach Olive
	SNACKS	Spice Lover's Cajun Eggplant
	DINNER	Korean Chili Pork
DAY5	**BREAKFAST**	Stuffed Up Bacon and Pepper
	LUNCH	Air Grilled Brussels
	SNACKS	Broccoli Maple Grill
	DINNER	Grilled Salmon Packets
DAY6	**BREAKFAST**	Mushroom Pepper
	LUNCH	Ginger Salmon with Cucumber Lime Sauce
	SNACKS	Eggplant and Tomato Meal
	DINNER	Orange Grilled Chicken Meal

DAY7	BREAKFAST	Kale and Sausage Delight
	LUNCH	Delicious Broccoli and Arugula
	SNACKS	Grilled Sweet Honey Carrot
	DINNER	Grilled Lemon-Garlic Salmon

Week 4

DAY1	BREAKFAST	Ninja Food Bean
	LUNCH	Cheddar Cauliflower Meal
	SNACKS	Crispy Brussels
	DINNER	Apricot-Chile Glazed Salmon
DAY2	BREAKFAST	Kale and Sausage Delight
	LUNCH	Grilled Salmon with Mustard & Herbs
	SNACKS	Cool Rosemary Potatoes
	DINNER	Delicious Grilled Honey Fruit Salad
DAY3	BREAKFAST	The Healthy Granola Bites
	LUNCH	Italian Squash Meal
	SNACKS	Honey Touched Bratwurst
	DINNER	Grilled Salmon Soft Tacos
DAY4	BREAKFAST	Energetic Bagel Platter
	LUNCH	Easy BBQ Roast Shrimp
	SNACKS	Tomato Salsa
	DINNER	Buttery Spinach Meal

DAY5	**BREAKFAST**	Grilled Apples with Bourbon and Brown Sugar
	LUNCH	Mushroom Tomato Roast
	SNACKS	Eggplant and Tomato Meal
	DINNER	Paprika Grilled Shrimp
DAY6	**BREAKFAST**	Stuffed Up Bacon and Pepper
	LUNCH	Teriyaki-Marinated Salmon
	SNACKS	Grilled Sweet Honey Carrot
	DINNER	Honey Carrot Dish
DAY7	**BREAKFAST**	Epic Breakfast Burrito
	LUNCH	Garlic Flavored Artichoke Meal
	SNACKS	Lovely Seasonal Broccoli
	DINNER	Grilled Fish Tacos

CONCLUSION

The Ninja Foodi Grill is the ultimate grilling appliance for food lovers and the best gift for the BBQ at home in the winter and rainy season. You will enjoy the yummiest food with the grill and this book will be a gem for the grill pro. The Ninja Foodi Grill allows grilling, baking, roasting, air frying or air crisping dehydrating and also cooks frozen food.

You will have what you want with this book and you will love the yummiest food. The Ninja Foodi Grill allows you the best food and taste of the char grilling. It will be loved by your all friends and family member as a grilling pro like a chef, so go grab the Ninja Foodi Grill along with this cookbook and start sharing your yummiest food.